CHILDREN'S
FIRST
DICTIONARY

© 1987 Autumn Publishing Ltd

Designed and produced by
Autumn Publishing Limited,
10 Eastgate Square, Chichester, England

Compiled by Rachael Jones
Illustrated by B. Pajić, Lj. Toskŏvić, B.Ban, J. Duval
This 1988 edition published by Derrydale Books, imprint
distributed by Crown Publishers, Inc.,
225 Park Avenue South
New York
New York 10003

Typeset by Words and Spaces, Rowlands Castle, Hampshire
Printed in Czechoslovakia
ISBN 0 517 64469 X
h g f e d c b a

CHILDREN'S FIRST DICTIONARY

DERRYDALE BOOKS
New York

abacus

An **abacus** is a wooden frame with rows of beads inside. It is used for counting.

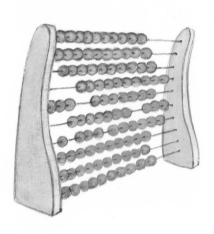

accordion

An **accordion** is a musical instrument. You press the keys and squeeze the box in and out to make a sound.

ace

An **ace** is a playing card that stands for number one. There are four aces in a pack of cards.

acorn

The **acorn** is the fruit of the oak tree.

acrobat

An **acrobat** performs exciting jumping and balancing acts. An **acrobat** often works in a circus.

actor/actress

An **actor** and an **actress** perform in plays, films, and on television.

adder

An **adder** is a small snake. It has a poisonous bite.

against

You might lean your bike **against** a wall.

ahead

The winner of the race was **ahead** of the others. Sometimes **ahead** can mean in front of you. Look **ahead** of you.

aircraft

An **aircraft** is any machine that can fly through the air.

airport

An **airport** is a place where an aircraft lands and takes off.

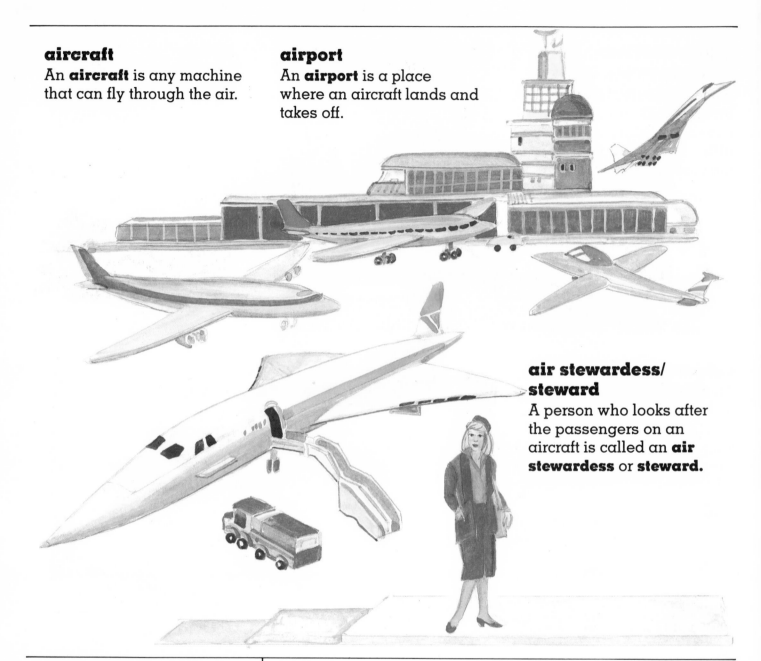

air stewardess/ steward

A person who looks after the passengers on an aircraft is called an **air stewardess** or **steward**.

alarm clock

An **alarm clock** can be set so the bell rings at a certain time. The **alarm** can wake you up in the morning.

album

Photographs, stamps, autographs and lots of other things can be put into an **album** for safe keeping.

alike
Things which look very much the same are **alike**. Brothers and sisters, and especially twins, often look **alike**. Baby animals from the same litter look **alike.**

alley
An **alley** is a narrow lane or back street.

alligator
An **alligator** lives by rivers. It is a reptile with a large mouth and many teeth, a long tail, and thick skin.

almond
An **almond** is a flat nut with a very hard shell.

alphabet
The set of letters used to make words is called the **alphabet**.

a b c d e f g h i

j k l m n o p q r

s t u v w x y z

ambulance
An **ambulance** takes sick or injured people to the hospital.

anaconda

An **anaconda** is a giant snake that lives in rivers in South America.

anchor

An **anchor** is a heavy hook that digs into the seabed to stop a boat or ship from drifting away.

angler

An **angler** is a fisherman who uses a rod, hook, and line to catch fish.

animal

An **animal** is any living thing which can move by itself. A child, horse, salmon and eagle, are all animals, but a tree or flower is not.

ankle
The thin part of the leg where it joins the foot is called the **ankle**.

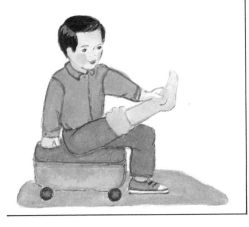

ant
An **ant** is a small insect. It lives in large groups with many other ants.

ant hill
An **ant hill** is the ants' nest. In some countries it can grow very large.

anteater
An **anteater** is an animal that eats ants. It has a long nose and a long sticky tongue.

antelope
An **antelope** is an animal that looks very much like a deer.

antler
The hard horns which grow out of a deer's head are called **antlers**.

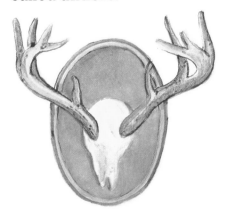

ape
An **ape** is a kind of monkey. Chimpanzees and gorillas are apes.

11

applaud

To **applaud** is to clap your hands together to show that you are pleased.

apple

An **apple** is a round fruit that is good to eat. Apples can be red, yellow, or green.

apricot

An **apricot** is a small, yellow fruit. Apricots are often made into jam.

apron

An **apron** is worn over your clothes in order to protect them from getting dirty.

aquarium

An **aquarium** is a building or tank where water animals and plants are kept. Some people keep fish in small aquariums in their homes.

aqueduct

An **aqueduct** is a bridge that carries water.

archer

An **archer** is a person who shoots with a bow and arrow.

ark

An **ark** is a large boat where animals live. It is said that a man called Noah built a huge **ark** to save his family and many animals from a great flood.

arm

The part of the body between the shoulder and the wrist is called the **arm**.

armchair

An **armchair** is a comfortable chair to sit in.

arrow

An **arrow** is a sharp, pointed stick which is shot from a bow. A sign to indicate directions may be in the shape of an **arrow**.

artist

An **artist** is someone who paints or draws pictures or creates other kinds of art.

ascend

To **ascend** means to go up or climb.

ash

An **ash** is a type of tree.

ash

The powder left by a fire is called **ash**.

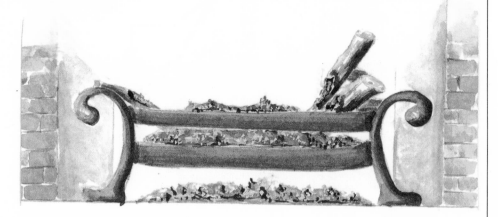

asleep

When you are not awake, you are **asleep**. The baby was fast **asleep** in the cot.

astronaut

An **astronaut** is a person who flies into space.

astronomer

An **astronomer** studies the stars and planets.

athlete

An **athlete** is a person who is good at running, swimming, or any kind of sport.

atlas

An **atlas** is a book of maps.

attic

An **attic** is a room underneath the roof at the very top of a house.

avalanche

An **avalanche** is a mass of snow, ice, and rock which slides down a mountain.

avenue

An **avenue** is a wide street often bordered with trees.

ax

An **ax** is a sharp tool used to chop wood.

axle

An **axle** is a rod which goes through the center of wheels that holds them in place.

baboon
A **baboon** is a large monkey.

baby
A **baby** is a very young child.

back
Your **back** is the part of your body from the neck to the end of the spine.

back
The **back** is the part behind the front of anything.

badger
A **badger** is an animal with gray fur. It has a white face with black stripes.

bag
A **bag** can be made of leather, plastic, cloth, or paper. It is used to carry things.

bake
To **bake** something is to cook it in an oven.

baker
A **baker** is someone who bakes bread and cakes.

bakery
A **bakery** is a shop where a baker works and where bread and cakes are sold.

balance
To **balance** means to put one thing on top of another so that it does not fall off.

balance

A **balance** is another name for weighing scales.

bald

To be **bald** means to have no hair - on your head for instance.

bale

A **bale** is a large bundle or package. You give a **bale** of hay to a horse, or you can pick a **bale** of cotton.

ball

A **ball** is a round object which can be bounced, thrown, hit, or kicked. Baseball, tennis, and football are all played with different types of balls.

ball

A **ball** is a large, grand dance. Cinderella went to a **ball**.

ballet

A **ballet** is a story told in music and dance.

ballet dancer

A **ballet dancer** is a person who dances in a **ballet**.

balloon

A **balloon** is a large bag filled with hot air or gas. It has a basket underneath in which people can ride.

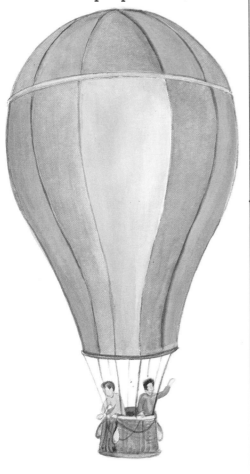

balloon

A **balloon** is made of thin, colored rubber. When it is filled with air it floats.

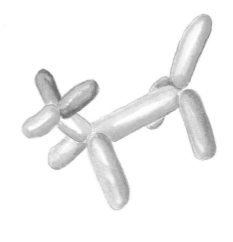

banana

A **banana** is a long, sweet fruit with a yellow skin that you peel off.

band

A **band** is a group of people who play musical instruments together.

bandage

A **bandage** is a strip of material that is put over a wound to protect it.

bangle
A **bangle** is another name for a bracelet.

banjo
A **banjo** is a musical instrument. It looks a bit like a short, round guitar.

banner
A **banner** is a kind of flag.

bar
A **bar** is a long piece of wood or metal.

bar
A **bar** is a block of chocolate or soap.

bar
A **bar** is a place that sells food and drinks at a counter.

barbecue
A **barbecue** is a meal cooked out-of-doors on an open fire.

barber
A **barber** cuts hair and trims men's beards.

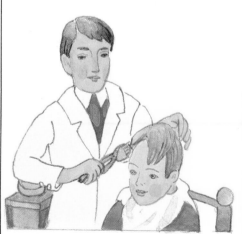

20

barge
A **barge** is a long, narrow boat with a flat bottom used on canals.

bark
The outer layer of trees is called the **bark**. Some animals enjoy eating the **bark** from trees.

barrel
A **barrel** is a round, wooden tub.

bat
A **bat** is a piece of wood used to hit a ball.

bat
A **bat** is a small flying animal that comes out at night.

beach

A **beach** is the land by the edge of the sea. It is usually sandy or covered with small stones.

bead

A **bead** is a small round object with a hole through the middle. Beads are used to make bracelets and necklaces.

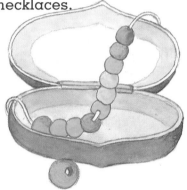

beak

The sharp, hard part of a bird's mouth is called the **beak**.

beam

A lighthouse or torch gives out a **beam** of light.

bean

A **bean** is a vegetable that is good to eat. Some beans grow in pods that can also be eaten.

bear

A **bear** is a large animal with thick fur. It can be brown, black, or white, depending on where it lives.

beard

A **beard** is hair that grows on a man's face.

beast

A **beast** is another name for an animal.

beaver

A **beaver** is an animal with very sharp front teeth, a broad flat tail, and webbed back feet. It builds its nest from twigs and mud in rivers and streams.

bed

When you go to sleep, you lie on a **bed**.

bedroom

A **bedroom** is a room where you sleep and sometimes play.

bee

A **bee** is a small flying insect that collects pollen from flowers to make honey. It has a sharp stinger in its tail.

beech

A **beech** is a type of tree.

beehive

A **beehive** is a nest where bees live and make honey.

beekeeper

A person who looks after bees in their hives is called a **beekeeper**.

beetle

A **beetle** is an insect. It has two pairs of wings. One pair protects the other pair which is used for flying.

23

belfry
A **belfry** is a tower where a bell is hung.

bell
A **bell** is a hollow piece of metal. A clapper strikes the metal to make a noise.

belt
A **belt** is a band worn around the waist made of leather.

bench
A **bench** is a long, wooden seat.

bend
To **bend** something is to make it curved.

bend
You **bend** down when you pick up something from the ground.

beret
A **beret** is a flat, soft, round cap.

berry
A **berry** is any small, round fruit with seeds. Some berries are poisonous.

bib
A **bib** is a piece of cloth or plastic used to protect a baby's clothes.

bicycle
A **bicycle** is a machine you can ride that has two wheels and pedals.

bikini
A **bikini** is a two-piece bathing suit.

bill
Another name for a bird's beak is a **bill**.

bill
A **bill** is a piece of paper that tells you how much money you have to pay for something.

billiards
The game of **billiards** is played on a long table with pockets at each corner and on two sides. There are three balls and you use a long stick, called a cue, to try to hit the balls into the pockets.

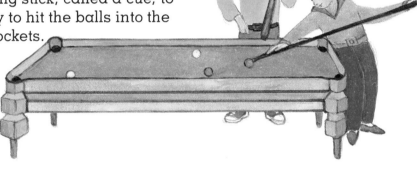

binoculars
You look through a pair of **binoculars** to make things in the distance appear closer.

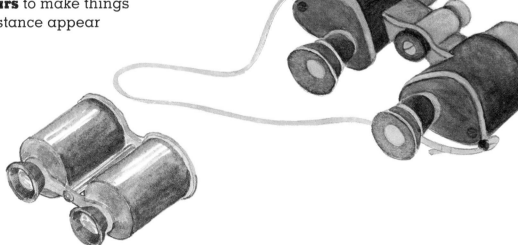

birch

A **birch** is a tree with a smooth bark.

bird

A **bird** is a feathered creature with wings, two legs and a beak. Most birds fly.

birthday

Your **birthday** is the day when you were born. In many countries children are given presents and have a party on their **birthday**.

bison

A **bison** is a wild ox. It grows a shaggy mane in the winter.

bite

To **bite** is to use your teeth to cut into something. You take a **bite** out of an apple.

black

Black is the darkest color. This rabbit is **black**.

blackberry

A **blackberry** is a small, soft, black berry that is good to eat.

blackbird

A **blackbird** is a common bird. The male is black, but the female is brown.

blackboard

A **blackboard** is a piece of black wood or stone that you can write on with chalk.

blacksmith

A **blacksmith** works in a forge and makes things out of iron.

blade

The flat, sharp, part of a knife is called the **blade**.

blade

You can also have a **blade** of grass.

blanket

A **blanket** is a large cover used to keep you warm.

blaze

To **blaze** means to burn brightly.

blazer

A **blazer** is a kind of jacket. It often has a badge on the top pocket.

blizzard

A very, very bad snowstorm with strong winds is called a **blizzard**.

blossoms

The flowers on a tree are called **blossoms**.

blot

A **blot** is a spot of ink.

28

blouse

A **blouse** is a piece of clothing worn by girls and women. It covers the top part of the body.

blow

To **blow** is to make air come out of your mouth.

blue

The color **blue** can be very dark or very light.

bluebells

A **bluebell** is a wild plant. It has tiny blue bell-shaped flowers.

boar

A **boar** is a wild pig.

board (bulletin)

A bulletin **board** is usually a flat piece of wood or cork. It can be fixed to a wall and you can pin your favorite pictures or letters on it.

boat

A **boat** can float on water. You can use oars and row a **boat** to make it move, or the wind can blow a **boat** along if it has a sail.

boil

To **boil** liquid is to make it so hot that it bubbles.

bolt

A **bolt** is a thick metal pin like a screw.

bolt

A sliding lock on a door is called a **bolt**.

bolt

To **bolt** is to run away quickly.

bone

The hard or rigid part of your body is made of **bone**.

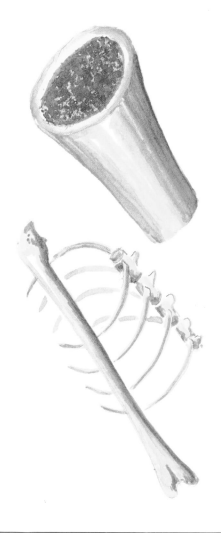

bonfire

A large fire built in the open air is called a **bonfire**.

bonnet

A **bonnet** is a hat with ribbons that tie under the chin.

book

A **book** has sheets of paper fastened together, with a cover around them. A **book** is usually filled with words and pictures.

bookcase

A **bookcase** is a set of shelves where books are kept.

31

boomerang

A **boomerang** is a thin curved stick. Because of its shape, it will come back to the person who throws it.

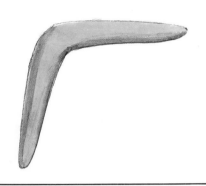

bottle

A **bottle** is a container for storing liquid. Bottles are made of glass or plastic and are narrow at the top.

boost

To **boost** is to help someone go up by lifting him from below.

boot

A **boot** is a strong shoe which comes above the ankle. Boots are made of rubber or leather.

bough

A **bough** is a large branch of a tree.

boulder

A **boulder** is a large rock.

bouquet
A bouquet is a bunch of flowers.

bow
A **bow** is a curved strip of wood with string joined to each end. An arrow is shot from a **bow**.

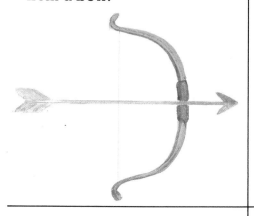

bow
A **bow** is used to play the violin. It is made of strong hairs stretched along a wooden rod.

bow
A **bow** is a type of ribbon and can be tied in a girl's hair.

bowl
A **bowl** is a deep round dish.

bowl
When you **bowl** you roll the bowling ball down the alley.

box

A container with a lid is
called a **box**.

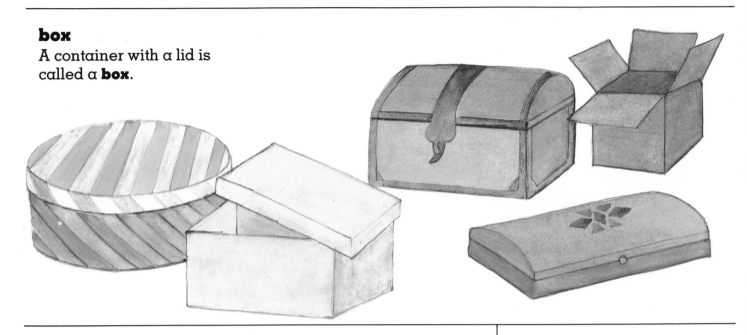

boxer

A **boxer** dog is a medium-
sized, smooth-haired breed
of dog.

boy

A **boy** is a male child. He
will grow up to be a man.

bracelet

A **bracelet** is a piece of
jewelry worn around the
wrist.

branch

A **branch** is the part of tree that grows out from the trunk.

bread

Bread is something you eat. You can buy it as a whole loaf, or cut up into slices.

break

To **break** something is to snap or smash it.

breakfast

The meal eaten first thing in the morning is called **breakfast**.

brick

A **brick** is an oblong block made of clay or mud that is used for building.

bricklayer

A **bricklayer** is someone who builds things made of bricks.

bride
On her wedding day, the lady getting married is known as the **bride.**

bridegroom
On his wedding day, the man getting married is known as the **bridegroom**.

bridesmaid
A **bridesmaid** is a girl or lady who helps the bride on her wedding day.

bridge
A **bridge** is a road or railway which crosses over something, such as a river or another road.

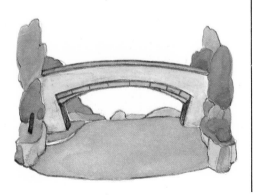

bridle
A **bridle** is put on a horse's head and nose. It is made up of leather straps. A bit goes into the horse's mouth and reins are attached to this.

brooch
A **brooch** is a piece of jewelry that is pinned to clothes.

brook

A small stream is called a **brook**.

broom

A **broom** is a stiff brush with a long handle. It is used to sweep up dirt.

brush

A **brush** has short, stiff bristles. Brushes are used to make hair neat, to sweep or scrub floors, and to paint.

bubble

A **bubble** is a small ball of air surrounded by liquid. You can make bubbles from soapy water.

bubblegum

A chewy candy that can be blown into bubbles is called **bubblegum**.

buck

Some four-legged animals **buck**. They stand on their front legs, and kick their back legs out.

buck

A male deer, hare, or rabbit is called a **buck**.

bucket

A **bucket** is a container with a handle but no lid.

buckle

A **buckle** is used on belts and straps to fasten the ends together. Some shoes fasten up with a **buckle**.

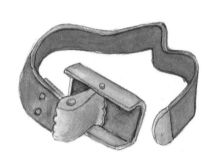

bud

A **bud** is a flower or leaf before it is fully open.

buffalo

A **buffalo** is a wild ox. It has horns and a small hump on its back.

bugle

A **bugle** is a brass instrument you blow into to make a sound.

build

To **build** is to make something by adding parts.

bulb

A **bulb** looks like an onion. It is planted in the ground. Flowers such as daffodils and tulips grow from bulbs.

bulb

A light **bulb** is a pear-shaped glass lamp. It is part of an electric light. When the electricity is switched on, the **bulb** lights up.

bull

A **bull** is a male cow, elephant, or whale.

bulldog

A **bulldog** is a breed of dog that is very powerful and brave.

bulldozer

A **bulldozer** is a large machine used to clear land.

bull's-eye

The middle of a target is called the **bull's-eye.**

bulrush

A **bulrush** is a tall plant that grows near water.

bump

To **bump** is to knock against something.

bump

You may trip over a **bump** on the ground.

bumpy

An uneven surface may be called **bumpy**.

bun

A **bun** is usually round and made of bread. You eat a hamburger in a **bun**.

bun

Hair coiled at the back of the head is called a **bun**. Grandmothers sometimes wear their hair in a **bun**.

bunch

A group of things tied together is in a **bunch**.

bunk beds

Two beds, one on top of the other, are called **bunk beds**.

buoy

A **buoy** is used to guide ships. It usually has a flashing light and floats on the sea. It is anchored to the sea bed to stop it from drifting away.

burden
A **burden** is a heavy load.

burst
If a balloon is blown up too much it will **burst.**

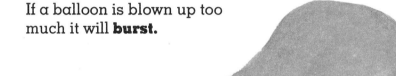

burr
A **burr** is the seed case of a plant. It is covered in tiny hooks which cling to people's clothes and animals' fur.

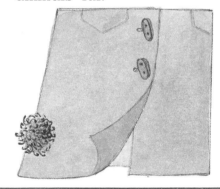

burrow
The hole in the ground where an animal lives is called its **burrow.**

bury
To **bury** something is to put it in a hole in the ground and cover it over. A dog will **bury** a bone.

off

bus

A **bus** has lots of seats and anyone can pay to travel on it. A **bus** stops at special places for people to get on and off.

bush

A **bush** is a plant that looks like a small tree.

butcher

A person who cuts up and sells meat is a **butcher**.

butter

Butter is a yellow food made from cream. It is used for cooking and spreading on bread.

buttercup

A **buttercup** is a wild-flower. It has shiny yellow petals.

butterfly

A **butterfly** is an insect with large wings. The wings can be white or brightly colored.

butterscotch

A hard candy made from butter and sugar is called **butterscotch**.

button

A **button** is sewn on to clothes to keep them fastened. It is usually round and made of plastic.

buttonhole

A **buttonhole** is a hole in clothes through which a button is inserted.

buy

To **buy** means to give money in exchange for something you want.

buzzard

A **buzzard** is a hunting bird like a hawk.

43

cab

The part of a truck, train, or bus where the driver sits is called the **cab**.

cab

A **cab** is a hired car with a driver. People can hire a **cab** to take them from place to place. Another name for **cab** is taxi.

cabbage

A **cabbage** is a vegetable with green leaves.

cabin

A **cabin** is a room on a ship.

cabin

The part of an aircraft where passengers sit is called the **cabin**.

cabin

A **cabin** is a small wooden hut.

cactus
A **cactus** is a plant that grows in hot, dry countries and does not need much water.

café
A **café** is a place where you can buy a drink and a meal.

cage
A **cage** is an enclosure used to keep animals. It has bars or wire across it.

cake
A **cake** is a sweet food made from flour, butter, eggs, and sugar.

calculator
A **calculator** is a machine that can do math problems very quickly.

calendar
A **calendar** shows the days, weeks, and months of a year.

calf
A young cow, elephant, or whale is called a **calf**.

calf
The back of the leg between the knee and ankle is the **calf**.

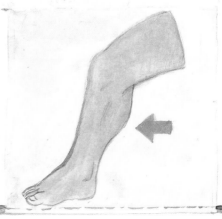

camel

A **camel** is a large animal with a long neck and long legs. It has either one or two humps and can travel many miles without food or water. Camels are used to carry people through deserts.

camouflage

To **camouflage** something is to hide it by making it look like its surroundings. Many wild animals, fish, and birds use **camouflage** to hide from other animals.

camp

A **camp** is a group of huts or tents where people live for a short while.

can

A tin container is called a **can**. It is usually sealed up and used to store food.

canal

A **canal** is a kind of man-made river. It goes straight from one place to another.

canary

A **canary** is a small, yellow bird. A **canary** sings very sweetly and is sometimes kept as a pet in a cage.

candle

A **candle** is a stick of wax with string through the middle. The wax melts as the string slowly burns, giving light.

candlestick

A **candlestick** is a holder for a candle.

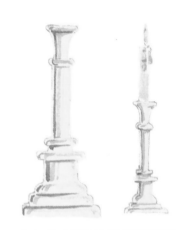

cane

A walking stick is sometimes known as a **cane**.

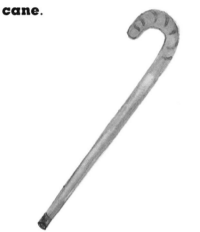

cane

The hard, woody stem of some plants is called **cane**.

canoe

A **canoe** is a light narrow boat. It has no engine and paddles are used to make it move.

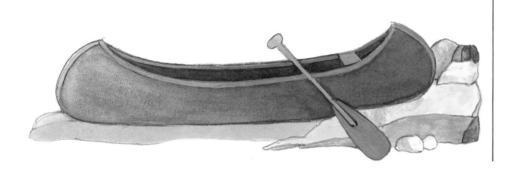

cap

A **cap** is a soft, flat hat.

cape

A **cape** is a short coat without sleeves.

capsule

The part of a spaceship that carries the astronauts is called the **capsule**.

captain

A **captain** is an officer in the army or navy. The leader of a team is also called a **captain**.

car

A **car** is a vehicle with wheels and an engine.

card

A **card** has a message and picture on it. You send cards on special occasions.

card

There are 52 playing cards in a pack. Each one has a picture or number on it.

cardboard

A very thick, strong paper is called **cardboard**. Boxes are sometimes made from **cardboard**.

cardigan

A **cardigan** is a knitted sweater that opens at the front.

cargo

Goods that are carried by ship, road, or air are known as **cargo**.

carnation

A **carnation** is a flower that smells very sweet.

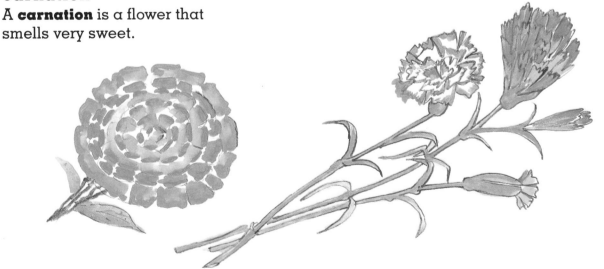

carols

Carols are the songs which we sing at Christmastime.

carp

A **carp** is a freshwater fish. A goldfish is a kind of **carp**.

carpenter

A **carpenter** makes things out of wood.

carpet

A **carpet** is used to cover the floor or stairs.

carrier pigeon

A **carrier pigeon** is a bird trained to carry messages from one place to another.

carrot

A **carrot** is a root vegetable. It grows in the ground and is long and orange.

cart

A **cart** is a vehicle with two or four wheels. It is often pulled along by a horse.

cart horse

A **cart horse** is a very large horse which is used to pull heavy loads on carts.

cartoon

A **cartoon** is a type of picture which makes things look funny.

cartoon

A **cartoon** is a film made from lots of drawings.

carve

To **carve** is to cut into pieces, usually meat.

carve

To **carve** is to cut shapes out of wood, with a sharp knife.

cash

Another name for paper money or coins is **cash**.

cassette

A **cassette** is a small container which holds a reel of tape. It can be used in a tape recorder to make sounds or in a video recorder to show a film.

castanets

Shell-shaped pieces of wood or ivory clicked together in the hand in time to music are **castanets**. They are used by Spanish dancers.

castle

A **castle** is a large house. It has very strong, thick, stone walls. You can also make a small **castle** from sand on the beach.

cat

A **cat** is a small furry animal often kept as a pet. Lions, tigers, and leopards are also part of the **cat** family.

catapult

A **catapult** is used to throw small stones through the air.

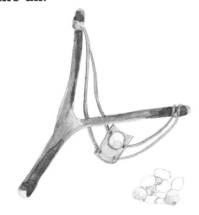

catch

To **catch** something is to get hold of it when it is thrown to you.

caterpillar

A **caterpillar** is a small creature which looks a little like a worm. A **caterpillar** turns into a butterfly or moth.

cathedral

A **cathedral** is a large, important church.

catkin

A **catkin** is a tiny blossom which hangs down in a bunch, usually from a willow or hazel tree.

cattle

The name for cows and bulls on a farm or ranch is **cattle**.

cauliflower

A **cauliflower** is a vegetable. It has a thick, white stalk with green leaves. Inside the leaves are small, hard white pieces called florets. The florets are the pieces that can be eaten.

cavalry

The **cavalry** is a group of soldiers in the army trained to fight on horseback.

cave

A **cave** is a large hole inside a mountain or under the ground.

ceiling

The top of a room is called the **ceiling**.

cellar

A **cellar** is a room under a building.

centipede

A **centipede** is a small, long creature with many legs.

chain

A line of rings joined together is called a **chain**.

chair

A **chair** is a piece of furniture to sit on.

chairlift

A **chairlift** is a series of chairs fixed on a cable. The cable runs from the bottom to the top of a mountain. The **chairlift** carries people up and down a mountainside.

chalk

The soft stick used to write on a blackboard is **chalk**.

chameleon

A **chameleon** is a small lizard that can change color to match its surroundings.

chauffeur

A person who is paid to drive a car for someone else is a **chauffeur**.

cheek

The round part of the face below the eyes is called the **cheek**.

cheese

Cheese is made from milk and is good to eat. There are many different kinds of **cheese**.

cheetah

A **cheetah** is part of the cat family. It has a spotted coat. The **cheetah** can run faster than any other animal.

chef
A person whose work is preparing and cooking food is a **chef**. A **chef** usually works in restaurants and hotels.

cherry
A **cherry** is a small, round, red or black fruit with a pit in it. Cherries can be eaten raw or cooked.

chest
A **chest** is a big, strong box.

chimney
The **chimney** is usually part of a house that takes smoke away from a fireplace.

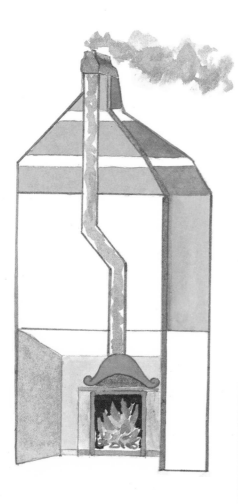

chest
The front part of the body between the shoulders and waist is the **chest**.
Your heart and lungs are in your **chest**.

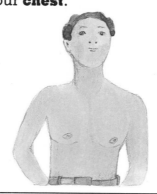

chestnut
The **chestnut** is a kind of tree. Some **chestnut** trees have hard, brown nuts also called chestnuts, which can be roasted and eaten.

chimpanzee
A **chimpanzee** is an ape with long arms and no tail. It is a very intelligent animal and can be trained to do many things.

chin

The part of the face under the mouth is the **chin**.

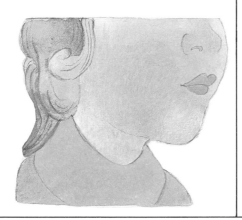

china

Plates, cups, and saucers made from thin pottery are called **china**.

chip

To **chip** something is to break off a thin piece of it.

chipmunk

A **chipmunk** is a small striped squirrel that makes its home in the ground.

chocolate

A sweet food made from cocoa and sugar is called **chocolate**.

choir

A **choir** is a group of people who sing together.

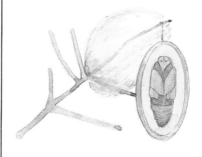

chrysalis

A **chrysalis** is the form taken by a caterpillar before it turns into a butterfly or moth.

church

A **church** is a building where people meet to worship God. Some weddings, christenings, and funerals take place in a **church**.

circle

A **circle** is a perfectly round shape, like a wheel.

circus

A **circus** is a show held in a big tent or building. Acrobats and clowns work in a **circus**.

city

A **city** is a very large town with many buildings and shops.

clap
To **clap** means to slap the palms of your hands together. People **clap** to show they have enjoyed something.

class
A **class** is a group of people who learn things together.

claw
A **claw** is one of the hard, sharp nails that some animals have on their feet.

climb
To **climb** means to go up. You can **climb** a mountain or **climb** up a ladder.

clock
A **clock** is a machine that shows what the time is.

cloud
A **cloud** floats high in the sky. It can be white, gray, or black. It is made of drops of water which often fall as rain.

clown

A **clown** is a person who wears funny clothes and makeup. A **clown** works in a circus and makes people laugh.

coal

Coal is a hard, black material that looks like stone and can be burned to give heat.

coat

A **coat** has long sleeves and is fastened at the front. It is worn over other clothes.

cobra

A **cobra** is a poisonous snake found in India and Africa.

cobweb

A **cobweb** is a fine, sticky net spun by a spider. The spider makes a **cobweb** to catch insects for food.

coconut

A **coconut** is the large, hard, round seed of a palm tree. Inside is a sweet white food and a white liquid which you can drink.

cocoon

A **cocoon** is the silky case spun by a caterpillar to protect it when it is a chrysalis.

cod

A **cod** is a large sea fish that is good to eat.

coil

To **coil** something is to wind it into circles.

coin

A **coin** is a piece of money made of metal.

collar

A **collar** is the part which goes round the neck of clothes.

collar

A **collar** is a band, usually leather, put around the neck of a dog or cat.

collie

A **collie** is a breed of dog that is kept for a pet and that can be trained to look after sheep. It has a long shaggy coat.

comb

A **comb** is used to make hair neat. It is made of plastic, wood, or metal and has thin points, called teeth.

comet

A **comet** travels through space. It seems to have a long ''tail'' behind it, which is made up of rocks and dust.

compass

A **compass** is an instrument for determining direction, which always shows the direction of "north."

cone

A **cone** is a shape which has a round base and comes to a point at the top.

cone

A **cone** is a fruit of the pine and fir tree. It has scales which open to let seeds out.

confetti

The small pieces of colored paper thrown at the bride and bridegroom at a wedding are **confetti**.

conifer

A **conifer** is a cone-bearing evergreen.

cook

A **cook** is a person who gets food ready to eat by heating it.

cookie

A **cookie** is small and flat and sweet. It is very nice to eat.

cornet

A **cornet** is a brass musical instrument that you blow.

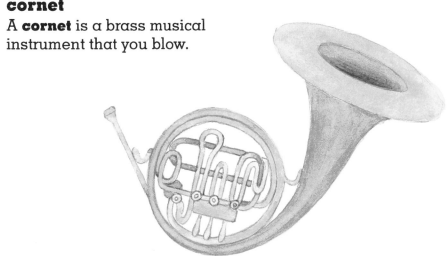

coronation

A **coronation** is the time when a king or queen is crowned.

cotton

The soft white part around the seeds of the **cotton** plant is called **cotton**.

cotton

Cotton is a light material made from the **cotton** plant.

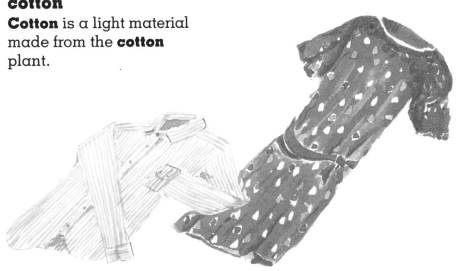

counter

A **counter** is the long table in a shop where you are served.

countryside

The **countryside** is the land away from towns where there are fields, woods, farms, lakes, and streams.

cow

A **cow** is a female bull. We drink cow's milk. The word is also used to describe a female elephant, whale, or seal.

cowboy

A **cowboy** is the man who looks after the cattle on a ranch.

crab

A **crab** is a sea creature with ten legs and a hard shell.

cracker

A **cracker** is a flat dry cookie that you eat with cheese and soup.

crate

A **crate** is a container used to carry bottles or other things which break easily.

crawl

To **crawl** is to move along the ground on hands and knees. A baby will **crawl** before it has learned to walk.

crayon

A **crayon** is a colored pencil or a stick of colored wax for drawing.

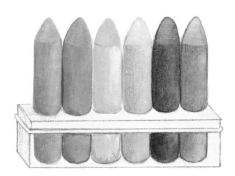

cricket

A **cricket** is a small brown insect that rubs its front wings together to make a chirping noise.

crocodile

A **crocodile** has short legs, a long body, and sharp teeth. It lives by rivers in some hot countries.

crocus

A **crocus** is a small flower with yellow or purple petals.

crow

A **crow** is a big, black bird. Farmers do not like crows because they eat their crops.

crumb

A **crumb** is a tiny piece of bread or cake.

cuckoo

A **cuckoo** is a bird that lays eggs in other birds' nests. The song it sings sounds just like its name.

cucumber

A **cucumber** is a long, green vegetable that is eaten raw, usually in salads.

cuff
The part of any clothes where the sleeve ends is called the **cuff**. You might have to fasten the **cuff** on a shirt or blouse.

cupboard
A **cupboard** is a piece of furniture with doors and shelves.

curl
A **curl** is a piece of hair twisted into a ring.

curl
A cat can **curl** up and sleep anywhere.

cutlery
Another name for knives, forks, and spoons is **cutlery**.

cymbal
A **cymbal** is a musical instrument. It has two brass plates which are crashed together to make a sound. A **cymbal** can also be hit with a stick.

daffodil

A **daffodil** is a yellow flower. The middle part of the petals is shaped like a trumpet.

daisy

A **daisy** is a small wild-flower. It has white petals and a yellow center.

dam

A **dam** is a wall built to hold back water.

dam

A **dam** is the name used for the mother of some four-legged animals.

dance

To **dance** is to move in time to music.

dandelion

A **dandelion** is a wild-flower. It is yellow and has a thick, green stalk.

dart

A **dart** is a sort of short arrow. You throw a **dart** at a dartboard to score points.

deck

The part of a ship where people can walk around is called the **deck**.

decorations

Things put around a room to make it pretty are called **decorations**. Special **decorations** are put up at Christmas and other holidays.

deer

A **deer** is a shy animal that usually lives in woods. It can run very quickly. The male **deer** have horns called antlers growing out of their heads.

dent

A **dent** is when the surface of something is pushed in.

dentist

A **dentist** is a person who takes care of your teeth.

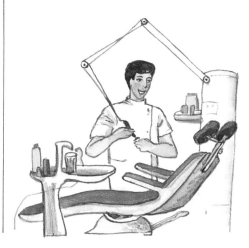

desert

A **desert** is a very dry place. Not many animals and plants can live in deserts. Some deserts are hot and sandy.

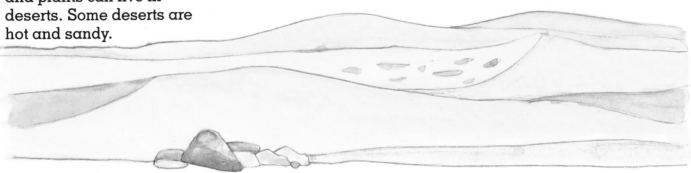

desk

A **desk** is a table where you can work. People read and write at a **desk**.

dessert

A **dessert** is something sweet which you eat at the end of a meal.

dial

A **dial** is a circle with numbers and letters on it. Some clocks and watches have dials.

diamond

A **diamond** shape has four sloping sides which are the same length.

diamond

A **diamond** is a very hard jewel. It looks like clear glass but it is very valuable. It sparkles in the light.

diary

A **diary** is a book where you write down the things that happen each day.

dictionary

A **dictionary** is a book where you can find out how to spell words, and what they mean.

dig

To **dig** means to make a hole in the ground. A dog will **dig** to find a bone he has buried.

dinghy

A **dinghy** is a small boat. It is moved either by rowing with oars, by a sail, or an outboard engine.

dinosaur

The **dinosaur** was a creature that lived millions of years ago. Some dinosaurs were small, but others grew to a great height.

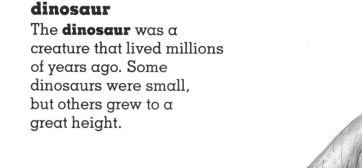

diver

A person who searches underwater for things is called a **diver**. He wears special underwater gear to do this.

doctor

A **doctor** will find out what is wrong when you are ill. He or she will try to make you feel better.

doll

A **doll** is a toy that looks like a person.

dolphin

A **dolphin** is a mammal which lives in the sea. It is not a fish but has warm blood, just like people.

dome

A **dome** is a shape like half a ball. Some roofs are dome-shaped.

donkey

A **donkey** looks like a small horse with long ears. It can carry heavy loads.

door

A **door** is a tall piece of wood, or sometimes glass, that fits into a wall in a building. It can be opened and shut so that people can go in and out.

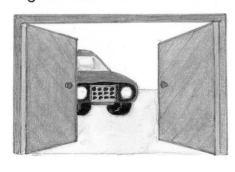

doughnut

A **doughnut** is a small, round cake. It is fried and dipped in sugar. Sometimes it has a hole in the middle.

dove

A **dove** is a bird that looks like a small pigeon. A **dove** makes a cooing sound.

dragon

A **dragon** is a monster that exists only in stories. It has wings and breathes fire.

dragonfly

A **dragonfly** is a brightly colored flying insect that lives near water.

drawer

A **drawer** fits into a piece of furniture such as a desk or chest of drawers.

dream

A **dream** is something you imagine while you are asleep.

drink

When you swallow liquid you **drink** it.

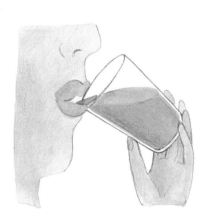

drip

To **drip** is to let liquid fall in drops.

drive

To **drive** is to make a machine, such as a car, move.

droop
Flowers **droop** when they need water. To **droop** is to hang down.

drum
A **drum** is a hollow musical instrument. It is hit with a stick to make a sound.

duet
When two people sing together it is called a **duet**.

dummy
A **dummy** is a model of a person. It is often used in shops to display clothes. Another name for **dummy** is mannequin.

dungarees
Dungarees are trousers made of cotton. Children and grownups wear **dungarees**. Another name for **dungarees** is blue jeans.

dungeon
A **dungeon** is a prison under a building.

dustcloth
The cloth that is used to wipe dust away is called a **dustcloth.**

eagle

An **eagle** is a bird with very large wings and big claws. It hunts small animals and uses its claws to carry its prey.

ear

The part of the head used for hearing is the **ear**.

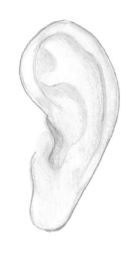

Earth

The name of the planet we all live on is **Earth**.

earth

Another name for soil is **earth**.

easel

An **easel** is a stand for holding a blackboard or a picture.

eel

An **eel** is a long, thin fish that looks like a worm.

elephant

An **elephant** is a very large and strong animal. It is gray and has a long nose which is called a trunk.

elf

An **elf** is a playful fairy that exists only in stories.

elm

An **elm** is a tall tree.

embroidery

Embroidery is a decoration made of colored threads that is sewn on to something.

emu

An **emu** is a large bird that lives in Australia. It cannot fly but it can run very fast.

encyclopedia

An **encyclopedia** is a large book or set of books. It tells you everything you need to know about a subject.

engine

An **engine** is a machine. It turns fuel into power and is used to make other machines work. All cars have engines.

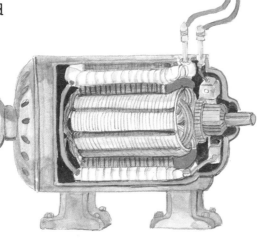

envelope

An **envelope** is a paper cover for a letter.

equator

The imaginary line around the middle of the Earth is called the **equator**. Countries near the **equator** are very hot.

escalator

An **escalator** is a moving staircase.

Eskimo
An **Eskimo** lives in the very cold parts of North America, Greenland, and Russia.

evening
The **evening** is the time at the end of the day when the sun goes down.

experiment
An **experiment** is a test to find out if an idea works.

explorer
An **explorer** is someone who searches around a place for the first time.

express
A fast train is called an **express**.

eye
The **eye** is the part of the face used for seeing.

eye
The small hole in a needle where the thread goes through is called the **eye**.

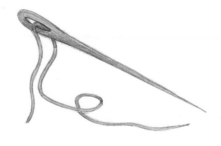

face

The **face** is the front part of the head. Your eyes, nose, and mouth are part of your **face**.

factory

A **factory** is a building where things are made.

fairy

A **fairy** is a tiny, magic person with wings that exists only in stories.

farm

A **farm** is land where crops are grown and animals are kept.

farmer

A **farmer** is a person who looks after the farm.

fawn
A **fawn** is a baby deer.

feathers
Birds are covered with **feathers**. **Feathers** keep birds warm.

fence
A **fence** is a wooden or wire enclosure.

ferry
A **ferry** is a boat that takes people from one side of a stretch of water to the other. Some ferries are big enough to carry cars as well as people.

fiddle
A **fiddle** is another name for a violin.

field
A **field** is a piece of ground used to grow crops or to play games on. Animals sometimes graze in a **field**.

fin
A **fin** is one of the thin, flat parts that stick out from a fish's body. A fish uses its fins to help it to swim.

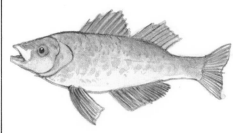

finger
One of the five separate parts of a hand is a **finger**.

fir

A **fir** tree's leaves look like thin needles. They do not fall off in the winter. The fruit of a **fir** tree is a **fir** cone.

fire

When something is burning, it is on **fire**.

fireplace

The part of a room where a fire is laid is called a **fireplace**.

firework

A **firework** is a paper tube filled with a powder. When it is set alight, the **firework** will bang, shoot into the sky, or send out colored sparks.

fish

A **fish** is any animal with scales and fins that always lives and breathes under water.

fishing

You use a net or rod and line when you go **fishing**.

fist

A closed hand, with all the fingers curled into the palm, is called a **fist**.

flag

A **flag** is a piece of material with a pattern on it. Every country has its own **flag**.

flamingo

A **flamingo** is a bird with very long legs. It also has a long neck and pink feathers.

flock

A group of sheep or birds that feed together is called a **flock**.

flood

A **flood** is a lot of water that covers land which is usually dry.

floor

The part of a building that people walk on is called the **floor**.

flour

Flour is made by grinding grains of wheat. It is used to make bread, cakes, and pastry.

flower

The part of a plant where the seeds grow is called the **flower**. It is usually the pretty, colored part at the top of the green stem.

fly
A **fly** is an insect with two wings.

fly
To **fly** is to move through the air using wings or in an aircraft.

foal
A **foal** is a baby horse or pony.

fog
Damp air that looks like smoke and is hard to see through is called **fog**.

food
Anything that you eat to help you grow is called **food**.

foot
The **foot** is the part at the end of the leg that you use to walk on.

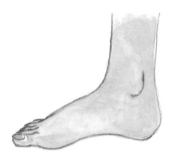

foot
Foot is a measure of length. It is the same as 12 inches.

forehead
The **forehead** is the part of the face between the hair and the eyebrows.

forest

A **forest** is a large number of trees growing together.

fork

A **fork** is a tool. It has three or four thin points called prongs or tines. Small forks are used to pick up food. A larger **fork** called a rake, is used in the garden.

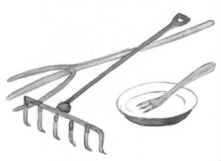

fort

A **fort** is a strong building built to protect a place against its enemies. Soldiers live in a **fort**.

fountain

When water shoots up into the air it is called a **fountain**.

fox

A **fox** is a wild animal that looks like a dog. It has red or gray fur and a long, bushy tail.

freckle

A **freckle** is a small, brown spot on the skin.

friend

A **friend** is someone who you like and who likes you.

fringe

A border of loose threads used to decorate something is called a **fringe**.

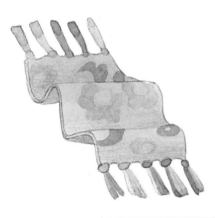

frog

A **frog** is a small animal that lives near water. It has long back legs and can jump well. Frogs have smooth, wet skins.

fruit

A **fruit** is the seed of a plant or the soft juicy part around the seed. Some fruits are good to eat.

frying pan

A **frying pan** is a pan used for frying foods.

fudge

A kind of soft, sweet candy, usually chocolate-flavored, is called **fudge**.

funnel

A **funnel** is the chimney on a ship or railway engine.

funnel

A tube with one very wide end is called a **funnel**. It helps you to pour liquid into a container.

fur

The warm hair that animals have is called **fur**.

furniture

The things inside a building which can be moved about, such as chairs and tables, are called **furniture**.

furrow

The straight, narrow rut made by a plow is called a **furrow**.

galleon

A **galleon** was a Spanish sailing ship used long ago.

galley

A **galley** was a boat used long ago. It needed many people to row it.

galley

A kitchen on a ship or aircraft is called a **galley**.

game

A **game** is something that you play with a set of rules.

garage

A **garage** is a building where a car or bus is kept.

garage

A place that fixes cars is called a **garage**.

garden

A **garden** is a piece of ground around a house. Flowers, fruit, and vegetables can be grown there.

gate

A **gate** is a door in a fence or wall.

geranium

A **geranium** is a plant with red, pink, or white flowers.

gerbil

A **gerbil** is a small, light brown animal with very soft fur. It has long back legs to help it dig holes in sand. Gerbils are often kept as pets.

giant

A **giant** is a very large person or animal. There are many fairy stories about giants. Some animals are called giants, like a **giant** panda and **giant** whale.

gift

A **gift**, also called a present, is something that people give each other, usually on special occasions.

gingerbread

A sticky cake that is flavored with ginger is called **gingerbread**.

giraffe
A **giraffe** is an animal with a very long neck and legs. It lives in Africa and eats leaves from tall trees.

glass
Glass is something hard that you can see through. Windows are made of **glass**.

glass
A **glass** is a cup made from **glass**. It has no handle. You drink liquids from a **glass**.

glasses
A pair of **glasses** is used to help people see better. Glass or plastic lenses are put into a frame.

glider
A **glider** is an aircraft with no engine. It has very long wings to catch the wind.

globe
A **globe** is a ball with a map of the world on it.

glove
A **glove** is a covering for your hand. It has a separate part for each finger and thumb.

gnome
A **gnome** is a kind of dwarf that exists only in stories.

goal

The **goal** is the pair of posts between which a ball is thrown or kicked to score a point in some games.

goat

A **goat** is an animal. A female **goat** is kept for its milk. A male **goat** has horns and a little beard under its chin.

go-cart

A **go-cart** is a small, four-wheeled cart that children can ride.

gold

Gold is a shiny, yellow metal. It is used mostly to make jewelry.

goldfish

A **goldfish** is a small, orange-colored fish. It is often kept as a pet.

golf

Golf is a game where a small, white ball is hit with sticks called clubs.

goose

A **goose** is a large bird that lives near water.

gooseberry

A **gooseberry** is a small green fruit that can be eaten. It grows on a thorny bush.

gorilla
A **gorilla** is a large ape. It has long arms and no tail.

grape
A **grape** is a small, green, red, or purple fruit. It grows in bunches on bushes called vines.

grapefruit
A **grapefruit** is a round, yellow fruit with a tough skin that looks a little bit like an orange. You peel the skin off and eat the segments.

grass
Grass is a green plant with flat, narrow leaves. It is eaten by many animals, such as horses and deer.

grasshopper
A **grasshopper** is a green insect. It can jump a long way. It makes a noise by rubbing its legs against its wings.

gravy
Gravy is a brown sauce. It is made from the juice of meat while it is cooking.

grin
A **grin** is a smile that shows the teeth.

grocer

A **grocer** keeps a shop that sells food, drinks, and other small things you need in the house.

guinea pig

A **guinea pig** is a small, furry animal. It has no tail and is often kept as a pet.

guitar

A **guitar** is a musical instrument. It has six or twelve strings. You strum the strings with your fingers.

gum

The **gum** is the hard, pink part of the mouth which holds the teeth.

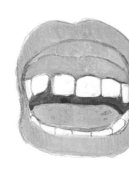

gum

Gum is a chewy candy that you do not swallow. Sometimes you can blow bubbles with **gum**.

gymnasium

A **gymnasium** is a place where you can exercise to keep fit. It is called a gym for short.

haddock

A **haddock** is an edible fish.

hair

The soft covering on the body, and especially the head, is called **hair**.

hairdresser

You visit the **hairdresser** to have your hair cut or styled. A **hairdresser** can curl hair by perming it, or straighten or color it.

halter

A **halter** is a rope or strap put around an animal's neck.

hammer

A **hammer** is a tool used to knock nails into wood.

hammock

A **hammock** is a bed that can be hung up by a string at each corner. It is usually made of canvas or rope.

hamster

A **hamster** is a small furry animal that is often kept as a pet. A **hamster** can store food in its cheeks.

hand

The part at the end of the arm is called the **hand**.

handkerchief

A **handkerchief** is a square piece of material used for blowing your nose.

hangar

A **hangar** is a large shed where aircraft are kept.

hanger

A **hanger** is made from wood or metal. Clothes are put on hangers and are hung in a closet.

harbor

A **harbor** is a safe place where ships can stay when they are not at sea.

hare

A **hare** looks like a big rabbit. It has large ears and can run very fast.

harness

A **harness** is a set of straps put over a horse's head and around its neck. When it pulls a cart it wears a **harness**.

harp

A **harp** is a large musical instrument. Strings are stretched down a frame and played with the fingers.

harvest

To **harvest** is to gather in the fruit or vegetables, that have been grown.

hawk

A **hawk** is a bird of prey which hunts and feeds on small animals.

head

The **head** is the part of a person or animal that contains the brain, eyes, ears, nose, and mouth.

heart

The **heart** is the part of your body which pumps blood.

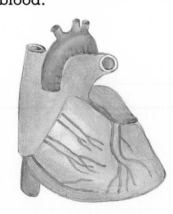

heart

A **heart** is a shape curved to look something like a real **heart**.

hedge

A **hedge** is a fence of bushes or low trees.

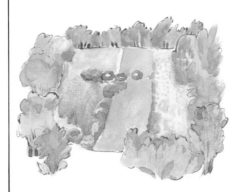

hedgehog

A **hedgehog** is a small animal that has sharp spines on its back. It rolls up into a ball to protect itself.

helicopter

A **helicopter** is a small aircraft which can go straight up into the air. It has special blades, called rotors, on its roof.

helmet

A helmet is a special hard hat that protects the head.

hill

A **hill** is ground that is higher than the land around it.

hippopotamus

A **hippopotamus** is a large, heavy animal that spends most of its time in the water. It lives in Africa.

hive

A **hive** is a bees' nest where they live and make honey.

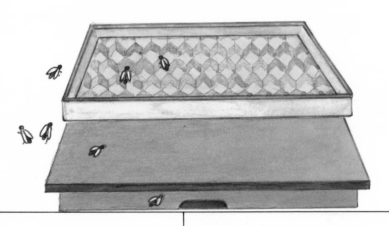

hoe

A **hoe** is a garden tool that is used to scrape out weeds.

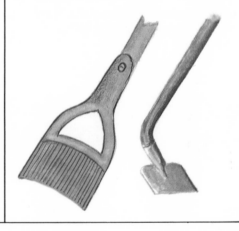

hole

A **hole** is an opening made in something,

holly

The **holly** tree has shiny, green, prickly leaves and red berries. At Christmastime you use **holly** as a decoration.

honey

Honey is a sweet, sticky food made by bees.

hoof

The hard part around a horse's foot is called a **hoof**.

hook

A **hook** is a piece of bent metal. It is used to catch hold of something or to hang things on.

hoop

A **hoop** is a large, round, plastic or wooden ring used in games. Jugglers often use hoops to do tricks.

horn

A **horn** is a musical instrument that you blow. The end is usually trumpet-shaped.

horn

A **horn** is a sharp bone that grows on the heads of some animals such as goats and bulls.

horse

A **horse** is a four-legged animal. It can be ridden or used to pull carts.

horseshoe

A **horseshoe** is a piece of iron that is shaped to fit under a horse's hoof. It protects the hoof and stops it from wearing down.

hose

A **hose** is a long length of tube that water can go through. Firemen use hoses to put out fires.

hospital

A **hospital** is where people go to be looked after when they are too ill to stay at home.

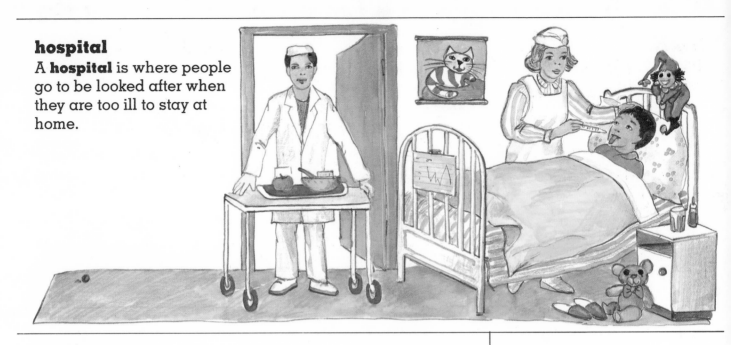

house

A **house** is a building where people live together.

human

A **human** is a man, woman, boy, or girl.

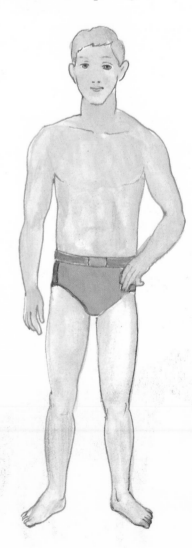

hyacinth

A **hyacinth** is a flower that has a very sweet smell. It grows from a bulb.

ice

Water that is frozen is called **ice**.

iceberg

An **iceberg** is a mass of ice floating in the sea.

ice cream

Ice cream is a cold, sweet food that tastes like cream. You can buy **ice cream** in many different flavors.

icicles.

Icicles are pointed spikes of ice that hang. They are formed by water dripping and freezing.

igloo

An **igloo** is a round house made from blocks of snow and ice. Some Eskimos still live in igloos.

illustration
An **illustration** is a picture.

inch
An **inch** is a measure of length.

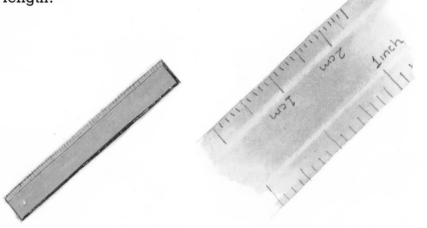

ink
Ink is a colored liquid used for printing or writing.

insect
An **insect** is a creature with six legs. Flies, ants, and butterflies are all insects.

instrument
An **instrument** is anything used to make music.

instrument
An **instrument** is another name for a tool. A dentist uses instruments to check your teeth.

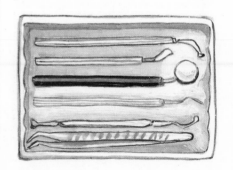

invitation
An **invitation** is a way of politely asking someone to do something or go somewhere.

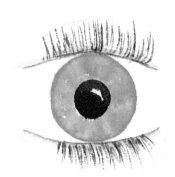

iris
The **iris** is the colored part of your eye.

iris
An **iris** is a plant with tall leaves and pretty flowers.

iron
An **iron** is an appliance used to press wrinkles out of clothing.

iron
Iron is a strong, heavy metal used to make many things.

island
An **island** is a piece of land with water all around it.

ivory
The white tusks on elephants are made of **ivory**.

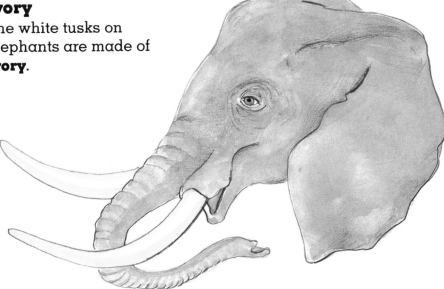

ivy
Ivy is a climbing plant that has shiny, dark green leaves.

jacket
A **jacket** is a short coat.

jam
Jam is a thick, sweet spread made by boiling fruit and sugar together.

jam
A crowd of people or cars which cannot move easily is called a **jam**.

jar
A **jar** is a glass or ceramic container.

jeans
Trousers made from strong cotton are called **jeans**.

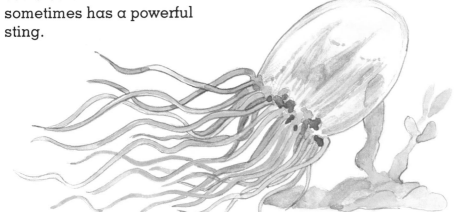

jeep
A **jeep** is a small, powerful, type of car.

jellyfish
A **jellyfish** is a transparent sea creature that sometimes has a powerful sting.

jet
A **jet** is an aircraft. Its engines are driven by a stream of hot gas.

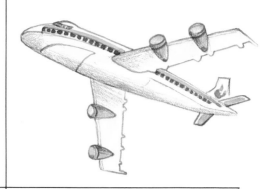

jet
A stream or shoot of water or gas coming out of a spout is called a **jet**.

jet
Hard, black stone which can be polished and made into jewelry is called **jet**.

jewel
A **jewel** is a precious stone.

jigsaw puzzle

A **jigsaw puzzle** is a picture on cardboard or wood cut into small shapes. To make the picture you fit the pieces together.

jockey

A **jockey** is a person who rides a horse in a race.

juggler

A **juggler** is a person who performs clever throwing, catching, and tricks.

juice

The liquid in fruit and vegetables is called **juice**. You squeeze the **juice** out of an orange.

jump

To **jump** is to leap suddenly into the air.

junction

A **junction** is a place where roads or railroad tracks meet or cross.

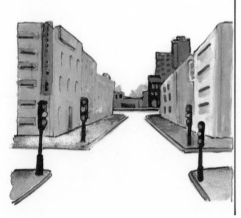

jungle

A **jungle** is full of trees, plants, and wild animals.It is usually a very hot place.

kangaroo

A **kangaroo** is an animal that lives in Australia. It has strong back legs and can jump very well. A female **kangaroo** has a pouch in which it carries its baby.

kennel

A **kennel** is a cage where a dog is kept.

kernel

A **kernel** is the part in the middle of a nut.

kettle

A **kettle** is a container with a lid, handle, and spout used to boil water.

key

A **key** is a piece of metal used to open a lock.

key

A **key** is a small lever which is pressed with a finger. Pianos and typewriters have keys.

kick

To **kick** is to move something with your foot.

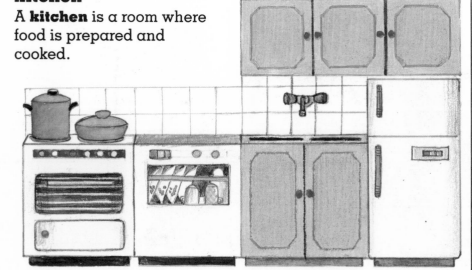

king

A **king** is a man who has been crowned. He rules a country.

kingfisher

A **kingfisher** is a small bird with brilliant feathers which lives near rivers.

kiss

To **kiss** is to touch someone gently with your lips.

kitchen

A **kitchen** is a room where food is prepared and cooked.

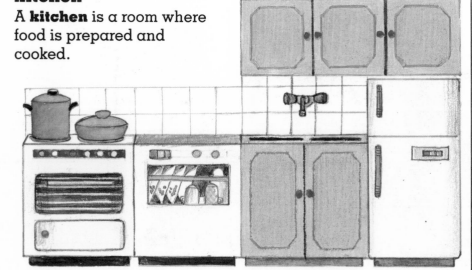

kite

A **kite** is a frame covered with paper. You fly it in the air on a windy day, attached to a long string.

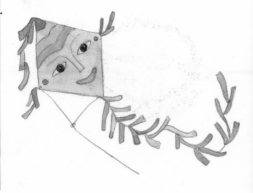

kitten
A **kitten** is a baby cat.

knee
The **knee** is the middle part of the leg that bends.

kneel
To **kneel** is to rest on the knees.

knit
You use two knitting needles and wool when you **knit**.

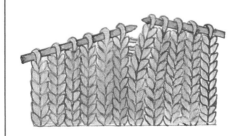

knob
A **knob** is a round handle on a door. Some drawers have knobs on them, too.

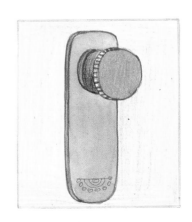

knot
A **knot** is where one or more pieces of material have been twisted together so that they do not come apart easily.

knuckle
A **knuckle** is one of the pieces of bone which you can feel on the top of your hand between your fingers and your wrist.

koala
A **koala** is a small bear-like animal that lives in Australia.

label

A **label** is a piece of card or sticky paper. It is put on something to say what it is, who it belongs to, or where it is going.

lace

Lace is thin, pretty material with a pattern of holes in it.

lace

A piece of thin cord used to tie shoes is called a **lace**.

ladder

A **ladder** is made of two long, thin pieces of wood or metal with short bars between them. You can climb up a **ladder** to reach a high place.

ladle

A **ladle** is a deep spoon used to serve soup.

ladybug

A **ladybug** is a red or yellow flying insect, with black spots on its back.

lake
A large area of water with land all around it is called a **lake**.

lamb
A **lamb** is a baby sheep.

lamp
A **lamp** is a light that can be moved to where it is needed.

lap
To run all the way around a racetrack is to run one **lap**.

lap
When a person sits down, the part from the person's waist to the knees is called the **lap**.

lap
To **lap** is to drink with the tongue, like a cat.

lark
A **lark** is a small, brown bird with a lovely song.

lasso

A **lasso** is a long rope tied so that there is a loop at one end. The loop can be made bigger or smaller.

lather

A foam of soapy bubbles is called **lather**.

laundromat

A **laundromat** is a place where people can wash and dry their clothes.

lawn

A **lawn** is the part of a garden covered with grass.

leaf

A **leaf** is one of the flat, green parts growing on a tree and other plants.

leak

A **leak** is when a liquid passes through a crack or hole in a container.

leash
A **leash** is a dog's lead.

leather
Strong material made from animal skins is called **leather**. Shoes, bags, and furniture can all be made of leather.

ledge
A **ledge** is a small shelf.

leek
A **leek** is a vegetable. It is long and white with green leaves.

lemon
A **lemon** is a yellow fruit with a sour taste.

lemonade
A drink made from lemons, sugar, and water is called **lemonade**.

leopard
A **leopard** is a member of the cat family. It has yellow fur with black spots on it.

leotard
A **leotard** is a piece of clothing worn by dancers and acrobats.

lettuce
Lettuce is a green vegetable that is eaten raw.

library
A **library** is a room or a building where lots of books are kept for people to use.

lifeboat
A **lifeboat** is a boat that goes out to sea to get people and other boats out of trouble.

light
Light is the power that lets things be seen. **Light** comes from the sun, moon, stars, flames, and electric lights.

lighthouse
A **lighthouse** is a tall building with a very powerful light at the top. The light flashes to warn ships at sea of danger.

lightning
The bright light that sometimes flashes in the sky during a storm is called **lightning**.

lily
A **lily** is a white plant. It is grown for its lovely flowers and sweet scent.

limb
A **limb** is a leg, arm, or wing.

lion/lioness

A **lion** is a member of the cat family that lives in Africa. The male **lion** has a mane of hair around its neck. The female is called a **lioness**.

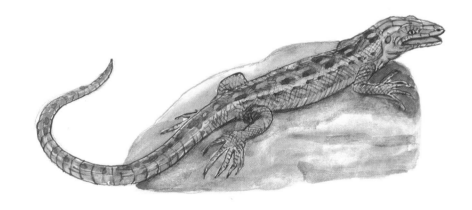

lips

Your **lips** are the outer part of your mouth. Together with your tongue and teeth, they help you to form words.

lizard

A **lizard** has a skin like a snake, four legs, and a long tail.

lobster

A **lobster** is a sea creature. It has a hard shell and two claws on its front legs.

lock

A **lock** is a fastening on a door or box. It is opened and shut with a key.

lock

A **lock** is a piece of hair.

locomotive
A **locomotive** is the engine that pulls trains.

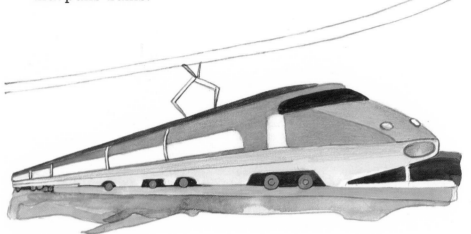

lollipop
A **lollipop** is a hard, sugary candy on a stick.

loop
A **loop** is a ring of metal, wire, or ribbon.

lunch
Lunch is the meal eaten in the middle of the day, between breakfast and dinner.

luggage
Another name for suitcases is **luggage**.

lung
The **lung** is one of the two parts inside your body that help you breathe.

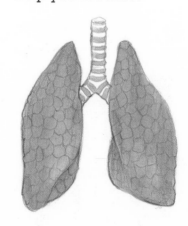

machine

A **machine** is something with several parts made to perform a certain job.

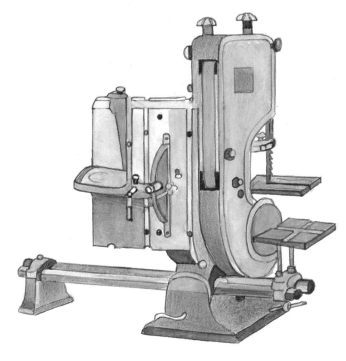

magician

A **magician** is a person who can do tricks of illusion.

magnet

A **magnet** is a piece of metal which makes other pieces of metal stick to it.

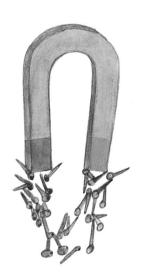

magnifying glass

A **magnifying glass** makes things appear bigger than they are.

magpie

A **magpie** is a bird with black and white feathers and a long tail.

mail

Letters and packages delivered by the post office are called **mail**.

mammal

A **mammal** is any creature that has warm blood and feeds its babies with its own milk.

mane

A **mane** is the long hair down a horse's neck or around a lion's neck.

manger

A **manger** is a box in a barn where food is kept for animals.

mantelpiece

A **mantelpiece** is the shelf above a fireplace.

map

A **map** is a diagram that shows where different places in the world are located.

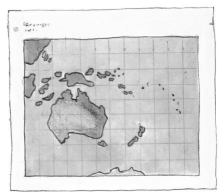

mask

A **mask** is something put over the face to hide it. You often wear masks on Halloween.

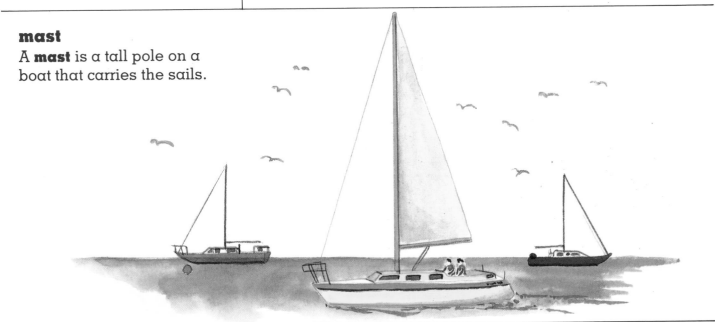

mast

A **mast** is a tall pole on a boat that carries the sails.

mattress

A **mattress** is the soft part of a bed that a person lies on.

maze

A **maze** is a set of paths and hedges that twist or turn. It is fun to try to find your way around a **maze**.

medicine

When someone is ill the doctor gives him **medicine** to make him feel better.

melon

A **melon** is a sweet, juicy fruit. It has a green or yellow skin.

melt

To **melt** something is to turn it into liquid when heated. Ice and snow **melt** when the temperature gets warmer.

mermaid

A **mermaid** is a storybook creature that is half woman and half fish. She lives under the sea.

microphone

A **microphone** changes sound into electricity. When someone speaks into a **microphone** his voice gets amplified and can be heard from a great distance.

microscope

A **microscope** makes tiny things appear much bigger when you look through it.

milk

The white liquid which mammals feed to their babies is called **milk**. People drink the **milk** that comes from cows.

mine

A **mine** is a place where coal, metal, jewels, or salt is dug out of the ground.

miner

A **miner** is a person who works in a mine.

mirror

A **mirror** is a piece of glass in which you can see objects reflected.

mistletoe

Mistletoe is a plant which grows white berries in the winter. It is used to decorate houses at Christmastime.

mitten

A **mitten** is a kind of glove. All the fingers go in one part, and the thumb goes in another.

moat

A **moat** is a ditch filled with water that surrounds a castle.

mole

A **mole** is a small, black, furry animal that spends most of its life under the ground.

monkey

A **monkey** is an animal that has long arms and legs and uses its feet and hands to climb. A **monkey** can also use its long tail to swing on branches.

moon

The **moon** is the satellite that moves around the Earth. It shines at night.

motor

A **motor** gives the power that drives machines, cars, boats, and lots of other things.

moth

A **moth** is an insect which looks like a butterfly. It usually flies at night.

motorcycle

A **motorcycle** is a machine that you can ride that has two wheels and an engine.

mount

To **mount** is to get onto something such as a horse or bike, to ride it.

mountain

A **mountain** is a very big hill.

mouth

The part of the face that opens for speaking and eating is called the **mouth**.

mow

To **mow** is to use a machine to cut grass.

mud
Mud is wet dirt.

mule
A **mule** is an animal whose mother is a horse and father is a donkey.

museum
A **museum** is a building where things are collected for people to see.

mushroom
A **mushroom** is a fungus that is shaped like an umbrella.

mussel
A **mussel** is a small sea creature that lives inside a pair of black shells.

124

nail

A **nail** is a sharp, pointed piece of metal. It is hammered into wood to hold the wood together.

nail

Your **nail** is the hard material that covers the end of each finger and toe.

narrow

Anything **narrow** is not very wide.

neck

The **neck** is the part of the body that joins the head and the body.

necklace

A **necklace** is a piece of jewelry that is worn around the neck.

needle

A **needle** is a very thin, pointed piece of metal used for sewing.

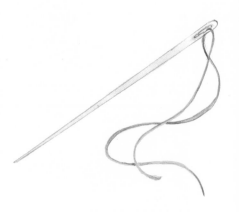

needle

A **needle** is a very thin pointed leaf. Pine trees have needles.

nest

A **nest** is where a bird lays and hatches its eggs. Many baby animals are born in nests.

newspaper

You read a **newspaper** to find out what is happening around you. The news is printed in a **newspaper**.

126

night

The time of day when it is dark is called the **night**. You are usually in bed asleep at **night**.

nightingale

A small, brown bird that sings at night is called a **nightingale**.

nose

The part of the face that is used for breathing and smelling is called the **nose**.

nurse

A **nurse** looks after sick and injured people.

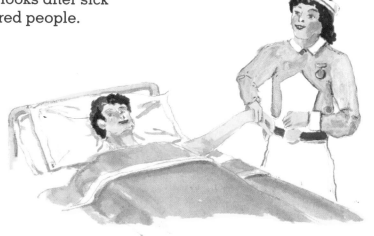

nut

A **nut** is a fruit with a hard shell. The piece inside the shell can be eaten.

127

oak

An **oak** is a kind of tree. The fruit of the **oak** is the acorn.

oasis

An **oasis** is a place in the desert where there is water and trees.

ocean

An **ocean** is a large area of saltwater. Oceans are found on Earth.

octopus

An **octopus** is a sea creature which has eight long arms.

office

An **office** is a room or building where people work. It has desks, telephones, and other business equipment in it.

ogre

In fairy tales, an **ogre** is a mean giant who hurts people.

onion

An **onion** is a round, white vegetable which has a very strong smell and flavor.

optician

An **optician** makes and sells eyeglasses.

129

orange

An **orange** is a round, juicy fruit. You remove the peel and eat the segments inside. The color of an **orange** is the same as its name.

orbit

When something moves around the sun or a planet in outer space its path is called an **orbit**.

orchard

An **orchard** is a place where many fruit trees grow.

orchestra

An **orchestra** is a group of people who play musical instruments together.

organ

An **organ** is a large musical instrument. It has keys like a piano which sound when air is pushed through a set of pipes.

ostrich
An **ostrich** is a large bird that cannot fly. It has a long neck and legs.

otter
An **otter** is a furry animal with webbed feet that lives near water.

outline
An **outline** is a line around the edge of something.

oven
An **oven** is used to bake and roast food.

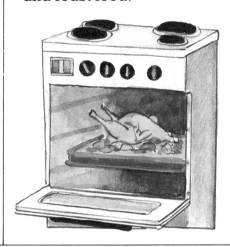

owl
An **owl** is a bird that hunts small creatures at night and that says, "WHOO!"

ox
An **ox** is a large animal like a cow or bull. In some countries an **ox** is used to pull a cart.

oyster
An **oyster** is a sea creature that lives inside a pair of shells. Sometimes a pearl is found inside an **oyster** shell.

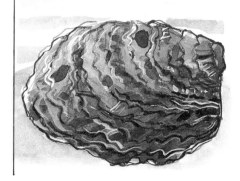

pack

To **pack** is to put things into a box or suitcase in order to move or store them.

pack

A group of dogs is called a **pack**.

package

A **package** is a small parcel.

padlock

A **padlock** is a lock joined to something by a metal loop. You use a key to open a **padlock**.

pail
A **pail** is a bucket.

paint
A liquid put on something to color it is called **paint**.

painter
A **painter** is someone who uses paint.

painting
A **painting** is a picture made with paint.

pair
A **pair** is two of a thing.

palace
A **palace** is a large house where a king or queen lives.

palm
The inside of the hand between the wrist and the fingers is called the **palm**.

palm tree
A **palm tree** is a tree with large leaves and no branches, which grows in hot places.

pancake
A **pancake** is made with flour, milk, and eggs. You usually eat pancakes for breakfast.

panda
A **panda** is a bearlike mammal found in China. It has black and white fur.

134

pansy

A **pansy** is a small, pretty flower.

paper

Paper is made from straw or tiny pieces of wood which are pressed and dried into very thin sheets. You can draw and write on **paper**.

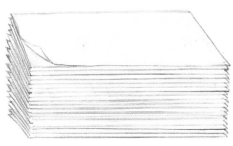

parade

When people in costumes march down the street with a band playing music, they are in a **parade**.

135

park

A **park** is a large garden where people can walk and play.

parrot

A **parrot** is a bird with bright feathers. Some parrots learn to repeat words that are said to them.

party

A **party** is when people get together and have fun. People usually celebrate their birthdays with a **party**.

patch

A **patch** is a small piece of material sewn over a tear to mend it.

path

A **path** is a narrow walk that people can use but cars cannot.

paw
An animal's foot is called a **paw**.

pea
A **pea** is a small round vegetable that grows inside a pod.

peach
A **peach** is a round, juicy fruit. It has a large pit and fuzzy skin.

peacock
A **peacock** is a bird with a long, bright tail which it can spread like a fan.

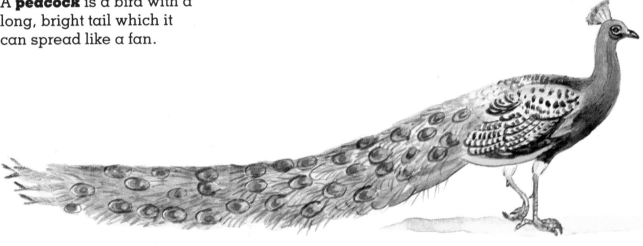

peak
The top of a mountain is called the **peak**.

peanut
A **peanut** is a tiny, round nut that grows in a pod underground.

pear
A **pear** is a juicy fruit.

pearl
A **pearl** is a small, shiny gem that can be found inside oyster shells. Pearls are often used to make jewelry.

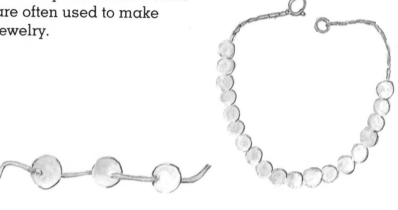

pebble
A **pebble** is a small stone.

pedal
To **pedal** is to push with a foot on a lever to make something work. When you ride a bicycle you **pedal** to make the wheels go around.

pelican
A **pelican** is a bird that lives on or near water. It has a very large beak where it stores food.

pencil
A **pencil** is used for drawing and writing. It is a thin, wooden stick which has lead inside it.

penguin

A **penguin** is a sea bird. It cannot fly but uses its short wings for swimming.

percussion instrument

Anything that is banged, hit, or shaken to make music is a **percussion instrument**.

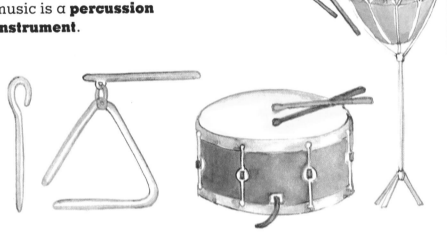

petticoat

A **petticoat** is clothing worn under a dress or skirt.

picnic

A **picnic** is a meal eaten outside.

pier

A **pier** is a long walkway built out over the sea.

pigeon

A **pigeon** is a very common bird. Tame pigeons can be taught to fly home from far away.

pillow

A **pillow** is a soft cushion that you rest your head on in bed.

pilot

A **pilot** is someone who flies an aircraft.

pineapple

A **pineapple** is a large fruit with a thick, lumpy skin. It grows in hot countries.

pipe

A **pipe** is a tube that takes liquid or gas from one place to another.

pirate
A **pirate** was a robber who long ago attacked ships.

pitchfork
A **pitchfork** is a tool used to lift hay. It has thin, sharp prongs attached to a long handle.

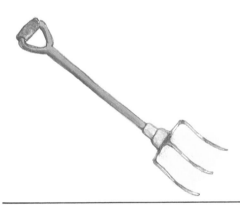

planet
A **planet** is a large body found in outer space that moves around the sun.

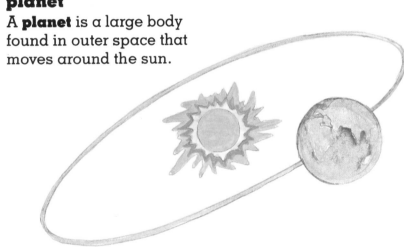

playground
A **playground** is a place out-of-doors where children can play safely.

pliers
A tool for bending wire or holding something is called a pair of **pliers**.

plow

To **plow** is to use a machine to dig and turn over the soil.

plum

A **plum** is a round purple fruit that has a pit in it.

plume

A **plume** is a long feather.

pod

A **pod** is a long seed case. Peas grow inside a **pod**.

polar bear

A **polar bear** has white fur and lives in cold places near the North Pole.

poodle
A **poodle** is a breed of dog. It has curly hair that is often cut very short.

poplar
A **poplar** is a type of tree. It is very tall and straight.

poppy
A **poppy** is a bright red flower. It often grows near corn.

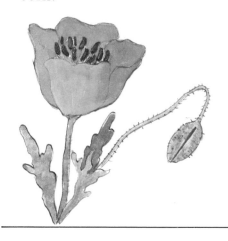

porpoise
A **porpoise** is a sea creature. It looks like a small whale.

porter
A **porter** carries luggage at a hotel or railway station.

potato
A **potato** is a vegetable that grows under the ground. It can be boiled, baked, roasted, or fried.

pumpkin

A **pumpkin** is a very large, round fruit. It has a hard yellow skin. You carve them to make jack o' lanterns at Halloween.

pupil

A **pupil** is the black spot in the center of the eye.

pupil

A **pupil** is a student.

puppet

A **puppet** is a doll that can be moved by strings or rods. Another kind of **puppet** has a body like a glove. You make it move by wriggling your fingers.

puppy
A **puppy** is a baby dog.

pyramid
A **pyramid** is a large stone building made by Egyptians long ago to hold the body of a dead ruler.
A **pyramid** has sloping sides that meet in a point at the top.

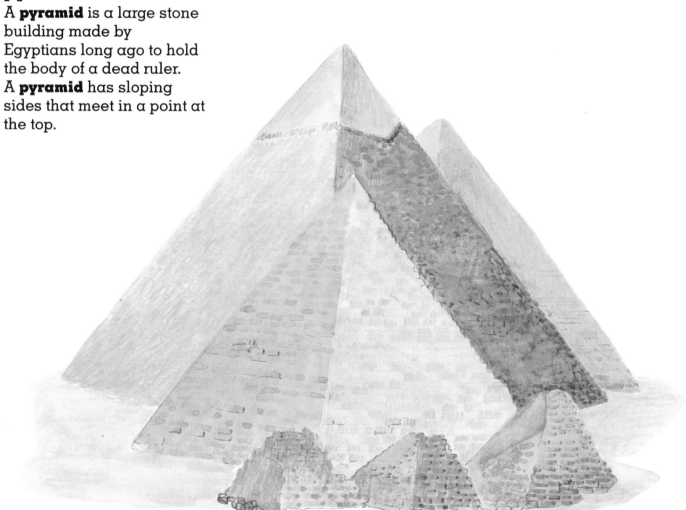

quarter

A **quarter** is one of the four equal parts that a thing can be divided into. It is also written as ¼.

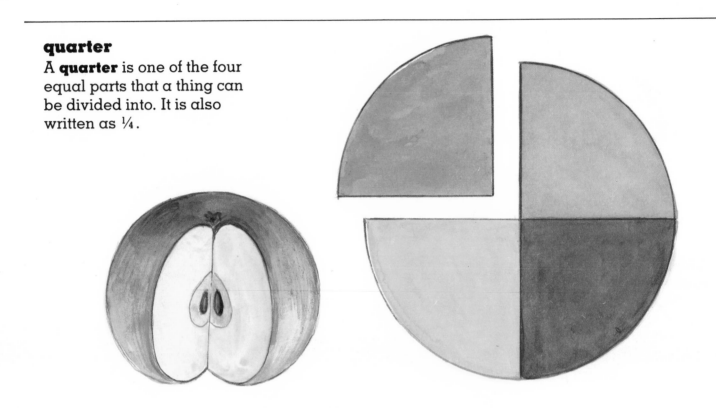

queen

A **queen** is a woman who has been crowned or who is a king's wife.

quill
An old-fashioned pen made from a goose's feather is called a **quill**.

quilt
A **quilt** is a warm cover that goes on top of a bed.

quiver
A **quiver** is a case where arrows are stored.

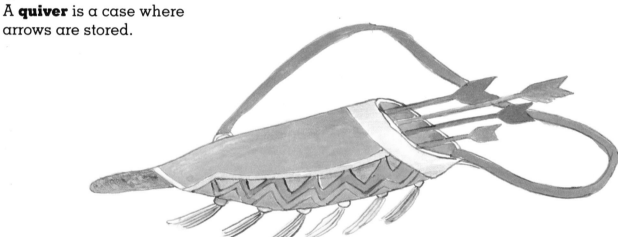

quiver
To **quiver** is to shake with fright.

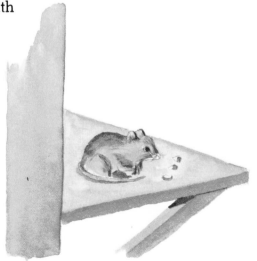

rabbit

A **rabbit** is a furry animal that digs a hole under the ground to live in. It has long ears and strong back legs.

race

A **race** is a test to find out who's the fastest.

rack

A **rack** is a shelf made from a set of bars.

radio

A **radio** is a machine that can pick up programs sent over the air so that people can hear them.

radish

A **radish** is a small, hard, red vegetable which grows in the ground and that can be eaten.

raft

A **raft** is a flat boat made from logs or planks tied together.

railway

A **railway** is a set of metal tracks that a train travels on.

rain

Water that falls in drops from clouds is called **rain**.

rainbow

A **rainbow** is a colored arc which appears when the sun shines through rain.

rake

A **rake** is a garden tool. It has a long handle and a spiked bar.

ranch

A **ranch** is a large farm with lots of cattle or horses.

raspberry

A **raspberry** is a soft, red fruit that is good to eat.

raven
A **raven** is a big, black bird.

ravine
A **ravine** is a deep, narrow space between cliffs.

rectangle
A **rectangle** is a shape with four straight sides, with its opposite sides being equal in length. A postcard is often the shape of a **rectangle**.

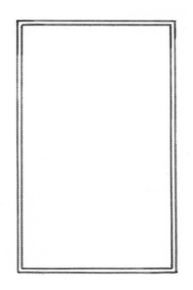

reeds
The hollow grass that grows near water is known as **reeds**.

reef
A **reef** is a line of rocks at or near the surface of the water.

reflection
When you look in a mirror you see an image of yourself. This is called a **reflection**.

refrigerator

A **refrigerator** is a cupboard where food and drinks are kept cold.

reindeer

A **reindeer** is a large deer that lives in cold climates.

reins

The thin straps that lead from a horse's bridle are called **reins**.

reptile

A **reptile** is an animal with cold blood. Its babies hatch out of eggs. Snakes, lizards, and turtles are all reptiles.

restaurant

A **restaurant** is a place where you go to eat and drink.

rhinoceros

A **rhinoceros** is a large, heavy animal that lives in Africa and Southern Asia. It has a horn on its nose.

rhubarb

The **rhubarb** plant has pink stalks which can be cooked and eaten.

ribbon

A **ribbon** is a long, thin piece of material used to tie back hair or as a decoration.

ribs

Your **ribs** are the curved bones of your chest. Your **ribs** protect your heart and lungs.

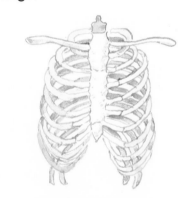

ring

A **ring** is a circle. A piece of jewelry worn on the finger is called a **ring**.

ringmaster

A **ringmaster** is the person who is in charge of the acts at a circus. He stands in the circus ring and announces the act.

rink

People go to ice skate or roller skate at a **rink**.

rip
To **rip** a thing is to tear it.

river
A river is a large stream.

road
A wide path with a hard surface that cars can travel on is called a **road**.

robin
A **robin** is a small bird with red feathers on its front.

rocket
A **rocket** is a firework that shoots into the sky.

rockets
Rockets fire a spacecraft into space.

roof
The part that covers the top of a building is called the **roof**.

root
The part of a plant which is in the earth is the **root**. Plants drink through their roots.

rope
A **rope** is a strong cord made of threads twisted together.

runway
The flat surface where airplanes take off and land is called the **runway**.

rye
A kind of grass grown by farmers is called **rye**. It is used to feed animals and its seeds are used to make bread.

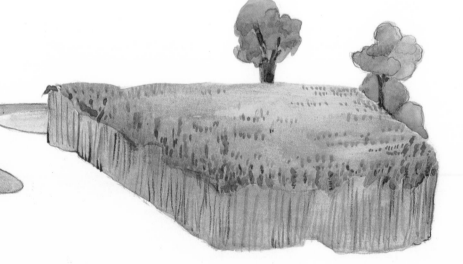

saddle
A **saddle** is the part of a bicycle that you sit on.

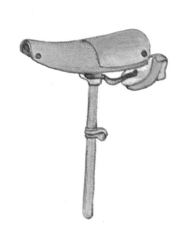

saddle
A **saddle** is a leather pad put on a horse's back for a rider to sit on.

safe
A **safe** is a strong box where money and jewels can be locked inside.

salad
A **salad** is a dish made from fruit or vegetables.

salmon
A **salmon** is a large fish. It has silvery sides and pink flesh.

sandal
A **sandal** is a light shoe worn in warm weather. Straps hold it onto the foot.

sandwich
A **sandwich** is made from two slices of bread and has fillings such as jelly, meat, or cheese in the middle.

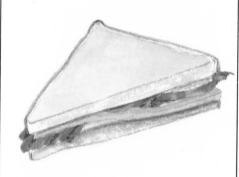

sardine
A **sardine** is a small sea fish.

saucer
A **saucer** is used to stand a cup on. It looks like a small plate.

saw
A **saw** is a tool. It has sharp points on one edge and is used to cut wood.

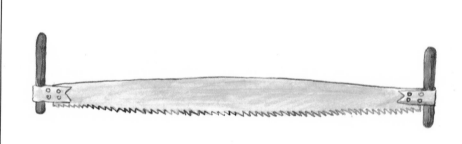

scale
A **scale** is a weighing machine.

scales
The small, thin plates of skin on a fish or snake are called **scales.**

scarecrow

A **scarecrow** is a figure made from wood and old clothes. It stands in a field and scares birds away from crops.

scarf

A **scarf** is a piece of material which covers the head or goes around the neck.

school

A **school** is a place where people go to learn.

scissors

A pair of **scissors** is a tool for cutting. It has two sharp blades and two handles which you fit your thumb and fingers into to open and close the **scissors** to cut things.

scowl

To **scowl** is to look angry.

screw

A **screw** is a kind of nail used to fasten things. It is put in a hole and twisted with a screwdriver.

sea

The **sea** is a large area of saltwater.

seagull

A **seagull** is a large, white sea bird.

searchlight

A **searchlight** is a strong beam of light that can be pointed in any direction.

seat

A **seat** is anything that can be sat on.

seaweed

Seaweed is a plant that grows in the sea.

seesaw

A **seesaw** is a plank balanced in the middle. When a person sits at either end, they can make the **seesaw** go up and down.

sew

To **sew** is to use a needle and cotton to join pieces of cloth.

shadow

A **shadow** is the black shape made when light falls onto something.

shaggy

To be **shaggy** is to have long, untidy hair.

shark

A **shark** is a fierce fish with lots of sharp, pointed teeth.

shawl

A **shawl** is a large piece of cloth worn around the shoulders or wrapped around a baby.

sheep

A **sheep** is an animal whose hair is turned into wool.

shelf

A **shelf** is a long piece of
wood fastened to the wall
that you can put things on.

shepherd

A **shepherd** is a person
who looks after sheep.

ship

A **ship** is a large boat that
makes long journeys over
the sea.

shoe

A **shoe** is a strong covering
that protects the foot.

shop

A **shop** is a place where
things are bought and sold.

sit

To **sit** is to rest on your bottom.

skate

To **skate** is to glide smoothly over ice or the ground wearing ice or roller skates.

skateboard

A **skateboard** is a long piece of wood or plastic on wheels. You push with one foot to make it travel quickly and then balance on it.

skeleton

The **skeleton** is the bony frame inside the body.

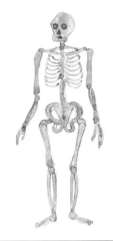

ski

To **ski** is to move over snow on two long, thin pieces of wood or plastic. You hold long poles to give you more balance.

skirt

A **skirt** is a piece of clothing worn by women and girls that hangs down from the waist.

sky

The **sky** is the space over our heads where the sun, moon, and stars can be seen.

skyscraper

A **skyscraper** is a very tall, modern building.

sleeve

The part of a piece of clothing that covers the arm is called the **sleeve**.

sleigh

A **sleigh** is used to travel over snow and is pulled by animals. It has strips of metal or wood instead of wheels.

slipper

A **slipper** is a soft shoe worn indoors.

smile

To **smile** is to turn up your mouth to show that you are happy.

snail

A **snail** is a small creature. It carries a shell on its back that it lives in.

snake

A **snake** is a creature with no legs and a scaly skin.

snorkel

A **snorkel** is a tube that a swimmer breathes through under water.

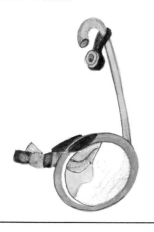

snowflakes

Small, thin, white pieces of frozen water that float down from the sky in very cold weather are called **snowflakes**.

soap

You wash with **soap** to make yourself clean.

socks

Socks are worn to keep your feet warm.

soup

Soup is hot, liquid food made from meat or vegetables.

spaceship

A **spaceship** is a machine that can carry people through outer space.

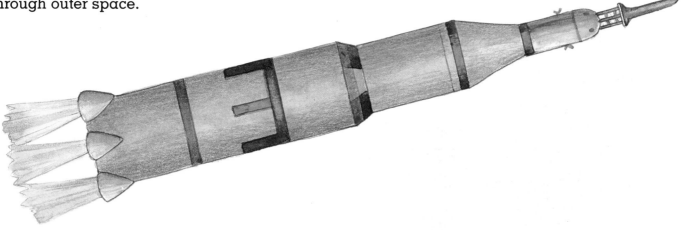

spaghetti

Spaghetti is a kind of pasta. It comes in long thin strands. When it is cooked it looks like soft string.

sparrow

A **sparrow** is a small, brown bird.

spider

A **spider** is a small creature with eight legs. Some spiders spin webs to catch their food.

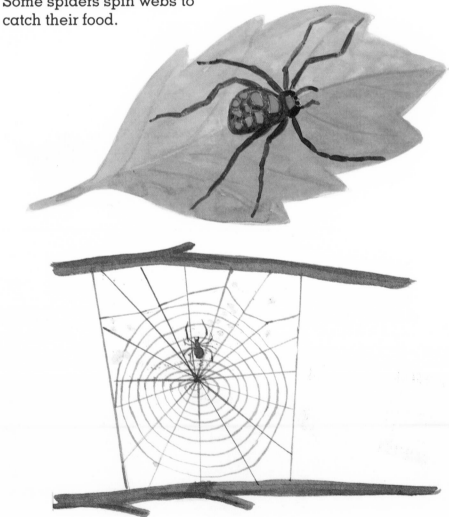

spire

A **spire** is a tall, pointed top of a church tower.

splint

A **splint** is a straight piece of wood or metal that is tied to a broken arm or leg to hold it firm.

sponge

A **sponge** is a thick, soft, rubber pad that soaks up water.

sponge

A **sponge** is a light, soft cake.

spoon

A **spoon** has a handle attached to a shallow dish. It is used for eating and stirring.

spout

The **spout** is the lip of a container where liquid comes out.

square

A **square** is a shape with four straight sides that are all the same length.

squid

A **squid** is a sea creature. It has eight short arms and two long ones.

squirrel

A **squirrel** is a small, furry animal with a long, bushy tail that lives in trees.

stable

A **stable** is a building where horses are kept.

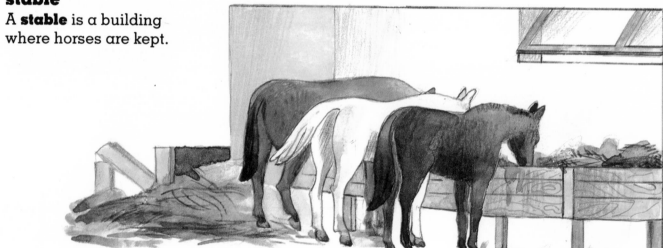

stamp

A **stamp** is a small piece of paper with a picture on one side. It is sticky on the back and is put on letters and packages to show that people have paid to send them.

166

statue

A **statue** is a metal or stone model of a person or animal.

steak

A **steak** is a thick piece of meat or fish.

stilts

A pair of **stilts** is made of two poles which help you walk high above the ground.

stirrups

Stirrups are the two metal foot rests which are attached by leather straps to a saddle.

stool

A **stool** is a seat without a back.

stork

A **stork** is a bird with a long neck and beak and very long legs.

strawberry

A **strawberry** is a soft, red fruit.

street

A **street** is a road with buildings on each side.

stretcher

A **stretcher** is made of canvas pulled across two poles. A sick person is carried lying down on a **stretcher**.

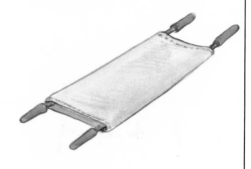

sty

A **sty** is where pigs live.

submarine

A **submarine** is a ship that travels under water.

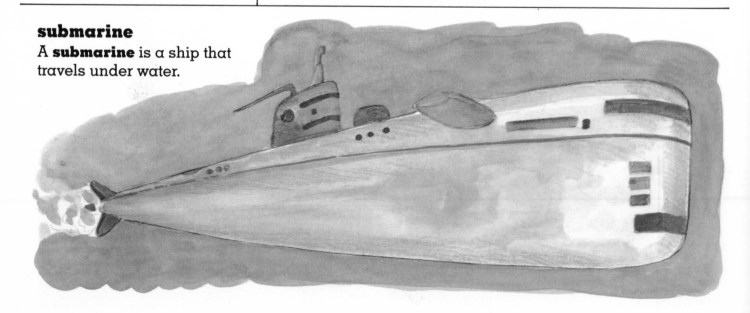

suitcase

You put clothes in a **suitcase** when you travel. You pack a **suitcase** when you go on vacation.

sun

The **sun** is in the sky. When the **sun** shines you feel warm. The **sun** rises early in the morning and sets in the evening.

swan

A **swan** is a large bird. There are many types of swans but the most common is white with an orange beak. Swans swim on ponds and lakes.

swim

To **swim** means to move in water. Many animals can **swim**. We **swim** by moving our arms and legs.

swing

To **swing** is to move backwards and forwards. You sit on a **swing** and make it go up in the air.

table

A **table** is a piece of furniture with a flat top.

tablecloth

A **tablecloth** is a piece of material used to cover a table.

tadpole

A **tadpole** is a tiny creature that lives in the water. It grows into a frog or a toad.

tail

The **tail** is the part at the end of something. Many animals have tails.

tambourine

A **tambourine** is a musical instrument. You can shake it or hit it with your finger to make music.

tangerine

A **tangerine** is a fruit that looks like a small orange. You peel it and eat the segments.

teeth

Teeth are the hard, white parts in your mouth. You use your **teeth** to chew food.

telephone

A **telephone** is an instrument that carries sound from one place to another. We use telephones to speak to each other.

telescope

A **telescope** is a tube with a lens at each end that makes things far away seem closer.

television

A **television** is a machine that can pick up signals sent through the air and change them into pictures and sounds.

tennis

A game of **tennis** is played on a court with a net across the middle. Players use rackets to hit a ball over the net to the other players.

tent

A **tent** is a shelter made of canvas that is stretched over poles. You sleep in one when you go camping.

thermometer

A **thermometer** is an instrument that tells you the temperature of something.

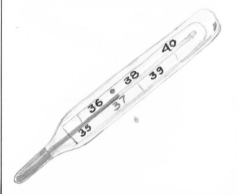

thimble

A **thimble** is a metal or plastic cover that protects your finger from a needle when you are sewing.

thistle

A **thistle** is a plant with prickly leaves and a purple flower.

thorn

A **thorn** is a sharp point on a plant's stem. Roses have thorns.

throne

A **throne** is a special seat for a king or queen.

throw

To **throw** is to make something travel through the air.

thrush

A **thrush** is a bird. It has a white front with brown spots.

thumb

The **thumb** is the short, thick finger on each hand.

173

tiger

A **tiger** is a big wild cat. It has orange and white fur with black stripes.

toad

A **toad** is a creature with a rough, dry skin. It looks like a frog but lives on land.

toast

Bread cooked until it is brown is called **toast**.

toboggan

A **toboggan** is a sled used for sliding down snow-covered hills.

toe

A **toe** is one of the five separate parts on each foot.

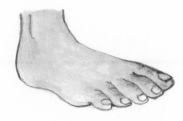

tomato

A **tomato** is a soft, red vegetable. It can be eaten raw or cooked.

tongue
The **tongue** is the soft, pink part that moves in the mouth.

tortoise
A **tortoise** is a slow-moving creature that has a hard shell on its back.

towel
A **towel** is a piece of material used to dry things.

town
A **town** is a place with lots of houses, stores, offices and other buildings. It is where people live.

tractor
A **tractor** is a large machine used on farms. It has big wheels and can pull heavy loads.

traffic
The word for the cars, buses, trucks and other things that travel on a road is **traffic**.

abcdefghijklmnopqrstuvwxyz

trampoline

A **trampoline** is a large piece of canvas joined to a metal frame by springs. You jump and bounce on a **trampoline**.

trapeze

A **trapeze** is a bar hanging from ropes on which acrobats in the circus perform tricks.

tray

A **tray** is a flat piece of wood or metal used to carry things on.

treasure

The word for gold, silver, and precious jewels is **treasure**.

tree

A **tree** is a tall plant with a thick stem, branches, and leaves.

trout

A **trout** is a fish that lives in rivers and lakes.

trowel

A **trowel** is a small spade with a short handle that is used for gardening.

trumpet

A **trumpet** is a musical instrument that you blow into to make sounds.

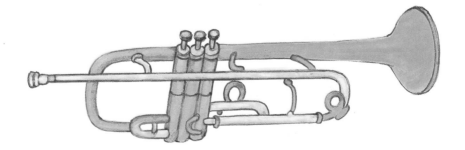

trunk

An elephant's long nose is called a **trunk**.

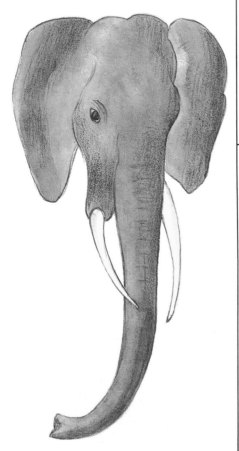

trunk

A **trunk** is a thick stem of a tree.

trunk

A **trunk** is a large case with a lid used to carry or store things.

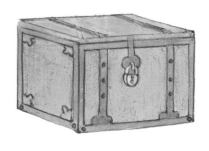

tulip

A **tulip** is a flower that grows from a bulb.

turkey

A **turkey** is a large game bird. You may eat **turkey** at Christmastime.

turret

A **turret** is a small tower on a castle.

turtle

A **turtle** is a sea or land creature that looks like a tortoise.

tusk

A **tusk** is a long, pointed tooth that grows from an elephant's mouth.

tweezers

A pair of **tweezers** is a tool for picking up small things.

twin

A **twin** is one of two children born to a mother at the same time. Twins usually look alike.

typewriter

A **typewriter** is a machine. It has keys which are pressed to print numbers and letters.

umbrella

An **umbrella** is made of cloth stretched over a frame. It is used to keep dry in the rain.

umpire

An **umpire** is someone who makes sure that players obey the rules of a game.

unicorn

A **unicorn** is an imaginary creature. It looks like a horse and has one horn sticking out of its head.

uniform

When everyone in a group wears the same clothes they are in **uniform**.

unwrap

To **unwrap** is to take the covering off something.

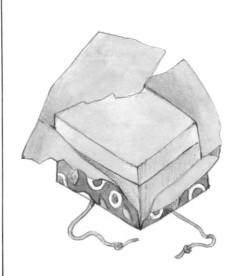

utensil

Any pot, pan, or tool used in the kitchen may be called a **utensil**.

valley
A **valley** is the low land that lies between hills.

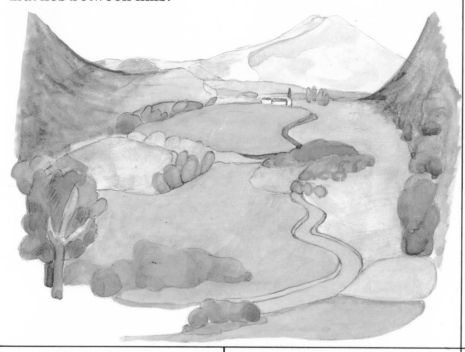

vase
A **vase** is a container used to hold flowers.

vegetable
A **vegetable** is the part of a plant that can be eaten.

vehicle
A **vehicle** is anything that takes people from one place to another on land.

veil
A **veil** is a thin piece of material used to cover the face.

veterinarian

A **vetinarian** is a person who looks after sick or hurt animals.

village

A **village** is a small place in the country where people live and that has few houses and shops.

violet

A **violet** is a small purple or white flower.

violin

A **violin** is a musical instrument. It has strings that are played with a bow.

volcano

A **volcano** is a mountain that contains hot liquid, gas, and ash.

wade

To **wade** is to walk through shallow water.

wagon

A **wagon** is a cart that is pulled by horses.

walkie-talkie

A **walkie-talkie** is a kind of two-way radio that can be used like a telephone.

wall

A **wall** is a fence made of bricks or stone.

wall

A **wall** is one of the sides of a room or building.

wallet

A **wallet** is a small, flat case used to carry money.

walnut

A **walnut** is a nut with a hard shell.

wand

A **wand** is a thin stick used by fairies, magicians, and witches to cast spells.

wash

To **wash** is to use soap and water to make something clean.

wasp

A **wasp** is a small insect that stings.

watch

A **watch** is a small clock on a strap worn on the wrist.

waterfall

A **waterfall** is a stream of water that falls from a high place to a low place.

weasel

A **weasel** is a small, furry animal with a long body.

web

A **web** is a sticky net spun by a spider to catch insects.

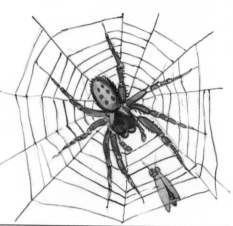

wedding

The celebration when a man and woman get married is called a **wedding**.

wedge

A **wedge** is a v-shaped object that is thick at one end and thin at the other.

weed

A **weed** is a wild plant that grows where it is not wanted.

weep

To **weep** is to cry.

whale

A **whale** is the largest sea creature.

wheel

A **wheel** is round and can turn.

wheelbarrow

A **wheelbarrow** is a small cart with one wheel at the front.

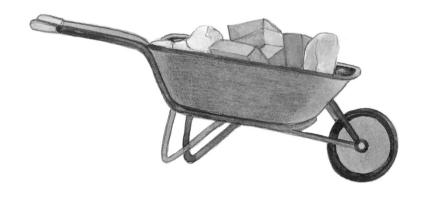

whisker

A **whisker** is one of the strong, stiff hairs that grows on the face. A cat has whiskers growing at each side of its mouth.

wig

A **wig** is a covering of false hair for the head.

wigwam

A **wigwam** is the word for an Indian's tent.

windmill

A **windmill** has four blades that turn when the wind blows and make the machinery work.

window

A **window** is an opening in a wall that lets in light.

wing

A **wing** is the part of a bird, insect, or an aircraft that helps it to fly.

witch

A **witch** is a woman in fairy tales who uses magic to do harm.

wizard

A **wizard** is a man who can do magical things. He can be good or bad.

wolf

A **wolf** is a wild animal that looks like a large dog.

woods

Trees growing near each other are called **woods**.

woodpecker

A **woodpecker** is a bird that uses its beak to make holes in tree trunks to catch the insects that live there.

wool

The thick, soft hair that covers a sheep is called **wool**. It is woven into strands and is used to knit garments.

workman

A **workman** is a man paid to work with his hands, tools, or a machine.

world

The Earth or the whole universe is called the **world**.

worm

A **worm** is a long, thin creature that burrows in the soil.

wren

A **wren** is a tiny, brown bird.

wrist

The **wrist** is the thin part of the arm where it joins the hand.

write

To **write** is to put words onto paper.

x-ray

An **x-ray** is a picture taken by a special machine that shows the inside of the body.

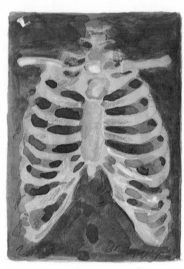

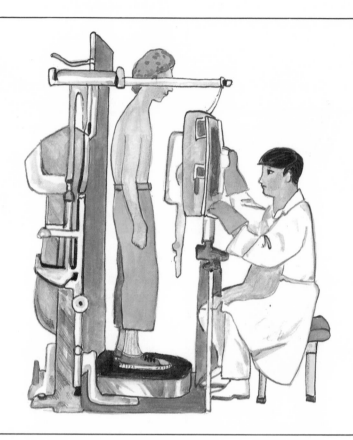

xylophone

A **xylophone** is a musical instrument. It has a row of bars that are hit with a small hammer to make a sound.

yacht
A **yacht** is a light sailing boat. It is often used for racing.

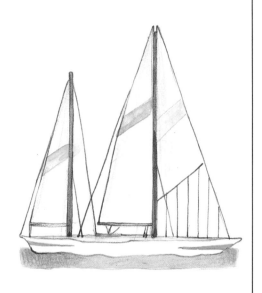

yawn
To **yawn** is to breathe in hard through an open mouth. It shows that you are tired.

yew
A **yew** is a tree with dark green leaves that stay on all year.

yogurt
A **yogurt** is a food made from sour milk. Sometimes it is sold with fruit mixed in.

yoke
A **yoke** is a long, curved piece of wood put over the head of two oxen to help them pull a cart.

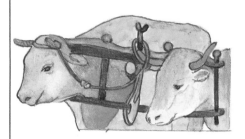

yolk
A **yolk** is the yellow part of an egg.

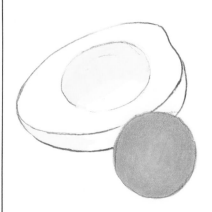

zebra

A **zebra** is a wild animal that looks like a horse with black and white stripes.

zero

Another word for nothing is **zero**. It can be written like this: 0

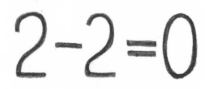

zigzag

A **zigzag** is a line with sharp turns in it.

zipper

A **zipper** is a fastener with metal or plastic teeth that joins together two edges of material.

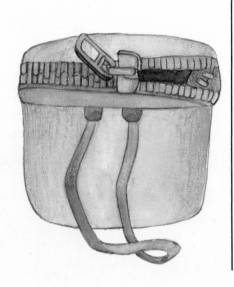

zoo

A **zoo** is a place where different animals are kept so that people can go and see them.